Carving
Fantasy & Legend
Figures in Wood

Shawn Cipa

FOX CHAPEL
PUBLISHING

Publisher
Alan Giagnocavo

Acquisition Editor
Peg Couch

Editor
Gretchen Bacon

Layout
Paul Cipa

Cover Design
Troy Thorne

Interior Photography
Shawn Cipa/Greg Heisey

ISBN 978-1-56523-807-7

To learn more about the other great books from Fox Chapel Publishing, or to find a retailer near you, call toll-free 800-457-9112 or visit us at *www.FoxChapelPublishing.com*.

Note to Authors: We are always looking for talented authors to write new books. Please send a brief letter describing your idea to Acquisition Editor, 1970 Broad Street, East Petersburg, PA 17520.

Printed in China
First printing

Dedication

To my father, Paul, who has always supported these carving endeavors of mine. I could not have completed this book without him. Also, to the rest of my family and friends, whom I love dearly.

Acknowledgments

Thanks to Fox Chapel for the opportunity to publish this book. Thanks to all the readers of my books for their much appreciated words of praise.

Table of Contents

About the Author

Shawn Cipa began carving in 1993 after his wife, Joanne, bought him a small set of palm tools for Christmas. Already possessing a solid background in art, it wasn't long before woodcarving became a driving passion in his life. He began by carving wood spirits, and soon after he tried his hand at Old Father Christmas. Although Shawn has carved many different subjects by commission, he admittedly prefers all things whimsical in nature. Walking sticks, canes, Santas, angels, and other mythical characters are just some of Shawn's repertoire.

Shawn comes from an artistic family and has experience in several art forms, including illustration, painting, and sculpture. Although working in most art mediums comes easy to Shawn, carving wasn't one of them. It was a daunting task to learn to sculpt by taking away, rather than by adding on, as in clay sculpting. However, perseverance has paid off.

Shawn was recognized as a national winner in Woodcraft Supply Corporation's 2000 Santa carving contest. He is also the author of *Carving Folk Art Figures* and *Woodcarving the Nativity in the Folk Art Style*, both available from Fox Chapel Publishing. Shawn does commission work from his website and provides pieces to many collectors internationally.

Shawn's other skills include carpentry, photography, and amateur astronomy. Shawn is also an accomplished musician of many years, a passion rivaling his love of the visual arts. He hopes to continue his carving endeavors with unending support from his family and friends, who have encouraged him.

Please feel free to contact Shawn by visiting his website at **www.shawnscarvings.com**. Shawn also contributes to the *Woodcarving Illustrated* message board at **www.WoodCarvingIllustrated.com**.

Introduction:
Wizards, Dragons, Faeries, and Mermaids

Creatures of lore permeate our psyche on a daily basis. From cave walls to the silver screen, these mythical beings have been around as long as man could begin to think creative thoughts. They have sprung from the deepest desires of men to make sense of nature and their place in it.

Some have such unnatural physical characteristics that there can be no question of their fictional origins. But others seem to have preceded mere imagination. Take the unicorn, for example. We all know what a unicorn is. Its majestic image is practically an icon of fantasy. But did you know that the unicorn has been mentioned in the Old Testament of the King James Version of the Bible several times? Almost every culture around the world has ancient references (and sightings) attributed to the unicorn. In fact, this elusive animal was believed to exist as recently as the late 1700s. So, who knows? Perhaps long ago there was a time when the unicorn did exist.

Another icon of fantasy is the wizard, or sorcerer. No doubt this fellow has been influenced by many literary characters, from King Arthur's Merlin to Middle Earth's Gandalf. Historical influences would include the ancient Celtic druids and medieval alchemists.

Ancient Chinese mythology places great importance on dragons. They were considered guardians of the universe. The Chinese view dragons as wise and benevolent creatures of the cosmos, whereas the Western image is of a terrible, evil serpent.

To sailors of the sixteenth and seventeenth centuries, the mermaid was a reality and a creature of which to be wary. Men who spent many months at sea were easily ensnared by her dangerous beauty.

The secret land of Faerie and all its magical residents are commonplace folklore in Britain, Scotland, and Ireland. Some still take faeries quite seriously.

Today, such fantastical creatures are decidedly more lighthearted, often being the subjects of countless fictional stories, whether they be written or portrayed in film. Many are even used as business logos by well-known international companies.

Fantasy and whimsy have always been important to me as a woodcarver and as an artist. I love to create my own ideas, and fantasy allows for such endeavors. Some of my ideas in this book are off the beaten path, while others have been inspired by certain characters found in fantasy literature. I encourage you, the reader, to use these patterns to help spur ideas of your own. Develop your own designs and color schemes once you are familiar with the techniques outlined in this book.

The carving projects in this book will appeal to beginning and intermediate carvers alike; some patterns are fairly simple, and others are more complex. Depending on your skill level, you may modify the pattern by adding or subtracting as much detail as you wish. For example, you may decide to omit the carved feather details around the Gryphon's neck. Painting them in is a good alternative. Conversely, you may decide to carve the scales on the mermaid or the sea horse, which I have merely painted. Some of the more complex designs do not necessarily take more skill to complete—only more time and patience.

I have strived to create designs that teach the average carver something about form and stylization yet are strategically compact enough to fit readily available wood stock. This is the dilemma of the woodcarver. It is a constant challenge to apply your ideas onto a somewhat limiting and an often unstable medium such as wood. Grain direction, availability of stock size, species of wood, and even the condition and sharpness of the tools all must fall into a balance in order to convey your thoughts into a tangible sculpture. This balance is what we all strive for; this is what makes us better carvers.

It is my sincerest hope that the average carver will find something new in these lessons, some spark that will light the fires of creativity that exists in all of us. So sharpen your tools, sharpen your mind, take your time, and enjoy!

—Shawn Cipa

Getting Started

Completing a woodcarving that satisfies your creative abilities and the opinions of those around you involves more than just "a knack for woodcarving." Making the right choice of wood and tools is equally important. Strike a good balance between techniques and talent, and you'll be setting yourself up for a great carving experience.

Wood choice

I used basswood for all of the carvings in this book. Basswood is probably the most common and most popular of carving woods in the United States. It is soft enough to carve comfortably but hard enough to hold great detail. It has virtually no grain to speak of, which makes it ideal for painting.

There are other species of wood that will work great for the projects in this book. Some hardwoods such as black walnut, cherry, and maple are very attractive, needing nothing more than a good oil finish. However, these three species in particular are considerably harder and are more difficult to carve than other hardwoods. Unless you are already familiar with carving these woods, I would suggest practicing with basswood first.

Butternut and mahogany, although considered hardwoods, are easy to carve. Butternut is particularly soft and has a very prominent and handsome grain. Mahogany carves wonderfully and has a beautiful natural color. These two woods are best finished with some type of varnish coat.

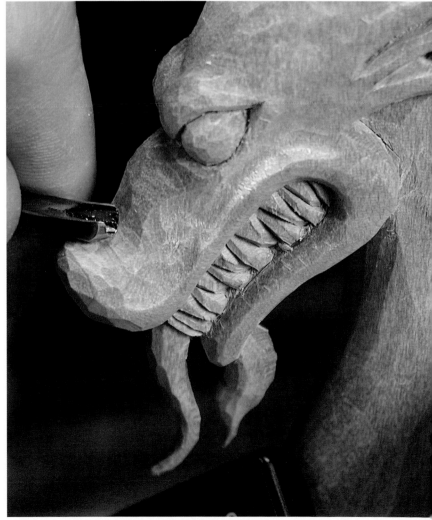

Basswood is probably one of the most popular woods for carving because it is easy to carve and it holds great detail.

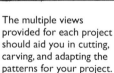

The multiple views provided for each project should aid you in cutting, carving, and adapting the patterns for your project.

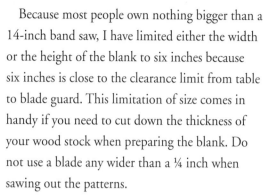

Using patterns

You will want to photocopy the patterns from this book to use as templates. Most of the patterns are actual size, so there is no need for enlargement. However, a few do require enlargement. I have marked the photocopy size on those patterns. Cut out the photocopied pattern and trace it onto the block of wood you have prepared, making sure that the front and side are lined up. Also, be sure to lay out the pattern lengthwise with the grain. The grain direction is marked on the pattern pages.

The dimensions for the wood blank are noted for each project. Several of the projects are only 2 or 2½ inches thick. In this case, I do not use the side patterns for cutting; instead, I use them for reference only.

Some of the project patterns in this book are fairly complex to cut on the band saw. If you are new to woodcarving, don't be intimidated or discouraged. Just take your time and plan your cut before plunging in. Be sure to cut out small bites at a time and leave extra wood around small protrusions. It will certainly help to practice bandsawing on scrap wood first, if you feel the need.

Because most people own nothing bigger than a 14-inch band saw, I have limited either the width or the height of the blank to six inches because six inches is close to the clearance limit from table to blade guard. This limitation of size comes in handy if you need to cut down the thickness of your wood stock when preparing the blank. Do not use a blade any wider than a ¼ inch when sawing out the patterns.

If you own or have access to a larger saw, feel free to enlarge the pattern and carve a bigger project! Of course, if you do not feel comfortable sawing out some of these patterns, have a more experienced person do it for you.

One tip when sawing: It saves a lot of time to knock off the hard corners wherever possible. To do this, tilt your band saw table to 45 degrees and carefully shave off the hard edges. Be careful not to pinch the blade during this procedure.

And finally, always remember to wear goggles and to practice safety precautions at all times!

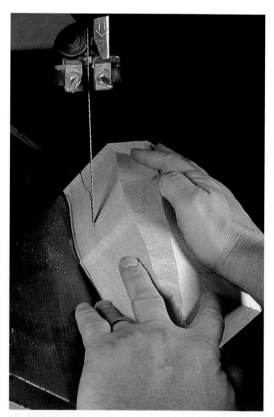

Hard edges can be quickly removed by tilting the band saw table to 45 degrees.

Using a vise

Due to the moderately complex pattern shapes of the projects in this book, I used a vise to hold the projects in place while I was carving. I strongly suggest the same for you, the reader. Most of the projects in this book are either too unwieldy or have too many delicate parts that could snap off to be handheld. Another reason to clamp the projects down is to free both of your hands. For the most part, hogging out excess wood is best accomplished with gouges rather than knives, and, for that process, you'll need to use both hands. Once the project is well underway, you can then hold it in your hands to add details.

Any carving vise or clamping system will do, either homemade or store bought. I mostly use a simple carpenter's vise that is built-in on my workbench, combined with bench dogs to wedge the project in place. If you will be using a common machine vise, be sure to line the inside of the jaws with some thin pieces of basswood; anything harder, and the carving will be marred.

Tools

As far as most of the projects in this book are concerned, the tool requirement is moderate. My personal course of action for these projects begins with putting the project in a vise, and then roughing out the project with a larger shallow gouge and, possibly, a mallet. Switching to medium-sized gouges and a variety of knives helps to work the piece into shape. Details are applied with small palm gouges and more knife work.

Learning to successfully sharpen your tools is an art unto itself—and it's practically half the battle when learning to carve. It took me several years to become comfortable with my own sharpening skills, and I tried many different stones and accessories. I finally bought a motorized wet grinder. I get an edge fast, but I have to be careful not to end up with a little nub for a tool. Fortunately, a wet grinder is not required to do a good sharpening job. I prefer to sharpen my knives by hand, leaving the grinder for the gouges. The job is easy with a pair of medium and fine ceramic stones. It would take a whole chapter or two to go over sharpening specifics, so I suggest purchasing a good sharpening book from your local bookstore or mail order carving supply store if you are not already accustomed to sharpening your own tools successfully.

A sharp tool is essential. You'd think this goes without saying, but there are so many beginners who struggle with a piece of wood only to give up in frustration. They blame themselves, thinking they don't have what it takes, when all along a dull tool was the culprit. To carve with the sharpest of tools is a joy that must be experienced to be appreciated.

A simple carpenter's vise paired with bench dogs holds the piece steady during the carving process.

Sheep's Foot

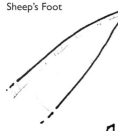

Spear Point

Pelican

Detail

The fishtail gouge is handy for making deep, incised cuts as well as smoothing out surfaces.

A word about knives

I prefer to have a few different types of knives on hand, which help me to get the job done more efficiently. A brief note on each one follows:

■ **Sheep's foot:** has a straight cutting edge. The most common of all carving knives. Good for roughing out or detail work, depending on the size of the blade.

■ **Spear point:** has a slightly curved cutting edge. Good for scalloping and slight hollowing. (My rough-out knife is a large, 2-inch spear point. I prefer this knife for roughing out because the rounded edge allows for more freedom of movement.)

■ **Pelican:** also has a curved cutting edge. Hollowed notch above the tip allows you to pare and scallop in a more detailed manner. Harder to find, but well worth it.

■ **Detail:** very small blade with a narrow point for detail work. Can have either a straight or a curved cutting edge. (I use a straight one.) Good for getting to hard-to-reach areas when mounted onto a long, thin handle.

The invaluable fishtail gouge

In my opinion, one of the most versatile carving tools you can own is the fishtail gouge. Because of its flared design, it can reach down into tight areas where undercutting is necessary. I often use this tool instead of a knife to define a deep, incised cut. The fishtail is also handy for smoothing out surfaces and minimizing "peaks and valleys" left by other tools. You can also flip it over to achieve a rounding effect on corners.

I would suggest having at least two different sizes of fishtail gouges on hand. A 1-inch-wide edge and a ½-inch-wide edge, both with a #5 sweep will cover most needs.

The pull saw

Based on a traditional Japanese design, the pull saw is a double-edged hand saw designed to cut on the pull stroke. This design makes it much easier to use than a conventional hand saw. I love this tool; it is a delight to use, and it cuts through any wood precisely and easily. You can purchase an inexpensive American version at any hardware store. (They usually have a fine tooth set on one side for crosscutting and a coarser set for ripping on the other side.) The pull saw is very thin, which makes it flexible, and leaves a very narrow kerf. It comes in handy when waste removal is needed at an unusual angle and where a band saw would be impractical or impossible to use. I used the pull saw several times for the projects in this book, and I would strongly suggest acquiring one; you won't regret the purchase!

When using the pull saw, remember that it mainly cuts on the pull stroke, so don't force it. The blade will cut easily—almost using its own weight to bite in. Despite the saw's large size, small cuts can be made with a minimal sweep. Because it is flexible, the blade can bend to reach an obscure angle if need be. I have also seen miniature versions of the pull saw in some hobby stores.

I find the pull saw to be easier to use than a conventional hand saw. It's also thin and flexible, and it leaves a very narrow kerf.

Alcohol and water

Sometimes basswood is not as soft as it should be, and sometimes the grade isn't so great, but it's all you've got. Often you have a lot of detail to carve right into the end grain, and, no matter how sharp your tool is, it still seems to tear the fibers instead of slice through them. For these instances, concoct a 50/50 mixture of water and isopropyl alcohol, put it in a spray bottle, and mist it lightly onto the area being worked. Let it soak in a few moments, and then spray it again. Start carving! The tool should glide through the stubborn wood much easier. I'm not sure how it works, but it does. I use it almost every time I need to carve end grain head-on. In this instance, it works wonderfully.

Crazy about glue

Cyanoacrylate, otherwise known as crazy glue or instant glue, is a very handy "tool" to have around. It's perfect for that desperate moment when you accidentally break off a fragile piece or chip out a chunk that should have stayed in place. Within moments of application, you're back in business! Try to stay away from the popular hardware store brands; these are often inferior in quality. Look instead for specialty brands found in woodworking stores, catalogs, or hobby shops. Instant glue is also excellent for reinforcing an otherwise fragile area. Simply apply the glue to the delicate area that you want strengthened and let it soak in. Within minutes the wood will be twice as strong as before.

A word of caution: cyanoacrylates are very volatile substances. The fumes will make your eyes and sinuses burn almost instantly, especially when closely bending over your work. Also, it will adhere anything to anything else—including your hand to the table. If this occurs, don't panic. Simply "peel" your hand or finger away from the surface it is adhered to in a rolling motion—don't pull! You can then peel off the dried glue from your skin or use a commercial thinner made especially for this type of glue. Thinner can be found in hobby and woodworking stores where the glue is sold. Better yet, wear gloves, a mask, and perhaps goggles, and use it in a well-ventilated area.

Before I paint, I usually apply a thin layer of boiled linseed oil mixed with mineral spirits. This application of oil helps to seal the carving and allows the paint to glide on more easily.

Painting and finishing

Every carver seems to have his or her own swear-by painting and finishing techniques. I have tried several that I like and dislike. Eventually personal experimentation leads to the method that suits you best. The method I will describe here has been applied to all of the carvings shown in this book.

I use acrylic paints as opposed to oils because they dry faster and they are easier to clean up. The cheap craft-type acrylic paints in the one-ounce plastic bottles are great to use. They are inexpensive and good quality paints, and there is a huge variety of colors from which to choose, which virtually eliminates the need to mix colors. These carvings, as fantasy characters, beg to be painted with creative colors. Use my choices as an example, but I encourage you to experiment with other colors as well. Remember: acrylics dry very fast (five to six minutes) and dry matte, not glossy.

Because you won't be spending much on paint, invest in good brushes. Really cheap ones are very hard to work with, and they fall apart. I would suggest a high-quality synthetic or sable brush. You will want at least four sizes: a ½-inch flat brush and a ¼-inch flat brush for blocking in colors, a ¼-inch round brush for getting into corners and some detailing, and a very small round brush for detailing. Make sure to always clean your brushes well after each use, especially when using acrylics. Brush conditioners work very well and increase the life of your brush.

The Basic Painting Technique

The key to applying color that lets the wood show through, yet has depth, is to progressively layer it in thinned coats. This requires a few steps.

I first apply a thin layer of boiled linseed oil thinned to a 50/50 mix with mineral spirits to the entire carving. Boiled linseed oil and mineral spirits are available at most hardware, woodworking, and craft stores. Let it soak in for a bit; then wipe off the excess with a clean cotton rag. Let the carving sit overnight, or at least for a few hours. The application of oil helps to seal the carving, which allows the paint to glide on more evenly over varying grain directions. It also allows different colors to blend together more smoothly; this is essential for layering. Be sure to wet your oil-soaked rags and dispose of them properly to avoid spontaneous combustion.

When applying the paint, be sure to have water on your brush as well as paint. I like to dip my brush in water, give it a shake, and load the brush with a dab of my chosen color. Apply it evenly, always keeping a wet edge on the surface of the carving while filling in an area with a single color.

Layering colors helps to give depth to the carving and improves the three-dimensional effect. Basically, you choose a base color for a given area. Then, use a darker hue of the same color for shadowed areas and crevices, blending it in with the base coat. In some cases, a lighter version may be desired for highlights. Just remember to keep each coat thin enough to see the wood through the paint.

The Basic Finishing Technique

After the paint has dried for at least an hour, the carving must be sealed. This step is done for two reasons: to brighten up the colors and, more importantly, to seal the carving for antiquing. If you skip this step and try to antique the carving without sealing first, you will end up with a big mess.

I have two methods of sealing. The first uses spray enamel; the second uses brush-on lacquer. For the first method, spray the carving with fast-drying, clear matte enamel. It must be matte! Follow the instructions on the can and give the carving two light coats a few minutes apart. If you don't like to use spray cans (sometimes they are very annoying to the senses), brush on a single thin coat of satin lacquer, such as Deft.

Let the carving dry overnight. When dry, the piece should still look matte. A dull sheen is okay.

The Basic Antiquing Technique

I like to antique my carvings. It pulls out the details and softens the pieces. To achieve this, I use an oil-based gel wood stain. Oil-based gel is good for two reasons. First, if your sealer got a little too thick somewhere and left a shine, the stain will help to dull that area a bit. Secondly, gel doesn't run. Whenever you use stain—gel or liquid—there is always some excess left in the nooks and crannies. When left to dry, liquid stain will eventually run out a bit and leave a little brown run mark. Gel stays put.

The color of the stain is up to you. I prefer to use anything titled "antique oak," "colonial," or "old oak." These colors appear to be dark brown but leave a warm, almost yellowed effect. Sometimes "fruitwood" is nice if you want an even more subtle effect.

Apply the stain with a disposable brush, working it into the deeper details. Slather it on! Then, wipe it all off with a cotton rag. Make sure you do this immediately because gel stain

dries quickly. You want the effect to be subtle. If you leave the gel on more than a minute, you will have a hard time getting it back off. I work quickly and usually apply the stain to the entire carving at once, but you may feel more comfortable doing these antiquing steps in sections. Let the wiped-off carving dry overnight, and your carving is complete.

Antiquing your carvings can help to pull out the details and to give the piece a softer effect.

The Wizard

The fantasy wizard comes in several types. I have chosen the wizened traveler, a keeper of secret knowledge. He appears as a fragile old man, but he has hidden strength and power. He is not unlike Middle Earth's Gandalf character, with his staff and long, flowing beard.

The Wizard is a good place to begin if you're new to carving fantasy figures. It is fairly simple, yet it requires a bit more aggression than a small whittling project. A vise or clamping system is required to carve the Wizard since he is 12 inches tall and almost 6 inches wide. You will need both of your hands when roughing out the piece, whether you use a mallet or not. Of course, you could carve him on a smaller scale, but I feel that would diminish the effect. The pattern provided will need to be photocopied at 120% to be the size of the piece I carved for this project.

My design is a fairly simple shape (unlike several of the projects in this book) and is a stylized form. Notice that the Wizard's left arm has been eliminated; it is assumed that the arm is hidden within the folds of his robe. I simply didn't need it to be there to achieve the look that I wanted. I consider this design to be somewhat free form, meaning that the guidelines are merely approximate. Liberty may be taken with this project when roughing out the blank. A slight shift in mass could change his whole attitude. Experiment!

The walking staff should be carved from a different species of wood to provide interest. I have chosen black walnut. Butternut is a good choice as well but may be more fragile. You may also choose a natural stick, bark still attached, from a tree branch. You may, of course, challenge yourself and carve the wizard and the staff all out of one piece; simply add the staff to the pattern when sawing out the blank.

If you are not accustomed to working this large, do not worry. Take your time, and don't try to rush the work. Enjoy as you go. It is always challenging and exciting to carve something new!

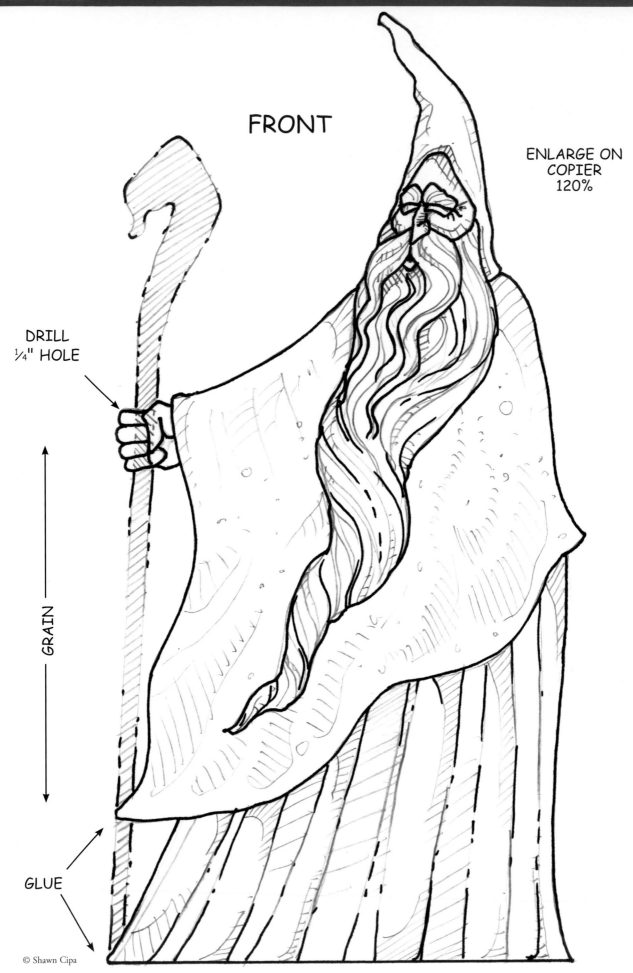

FRONT

ENLARGE ON
COPIER
120%

DRILL
¼" HOLE

GRAIN

GLUE

© Shawn Cipa

BACK

ENLARGE ON
COPIER
120%

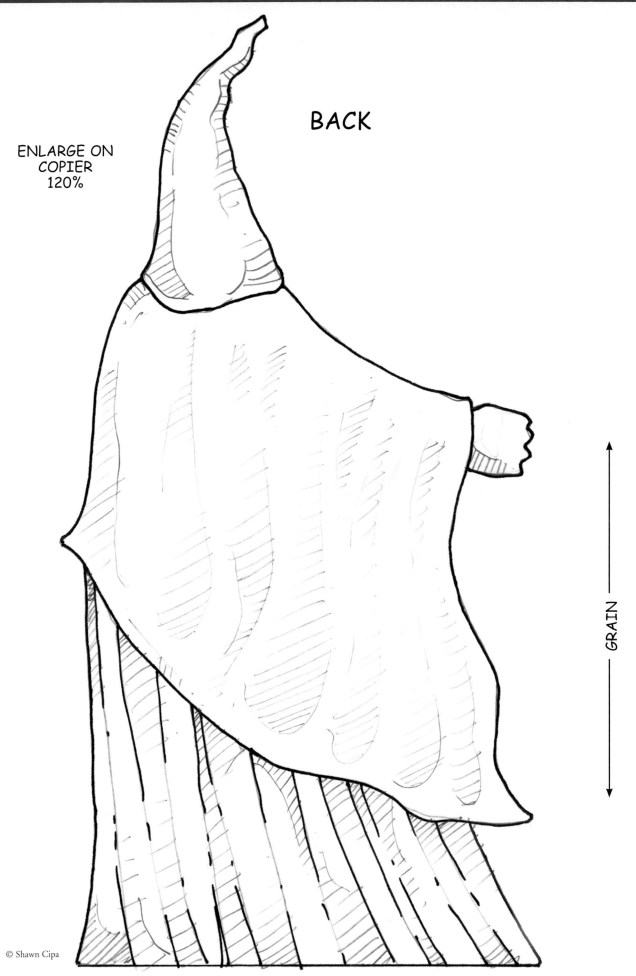

GRAIN

© Shawn Cipa

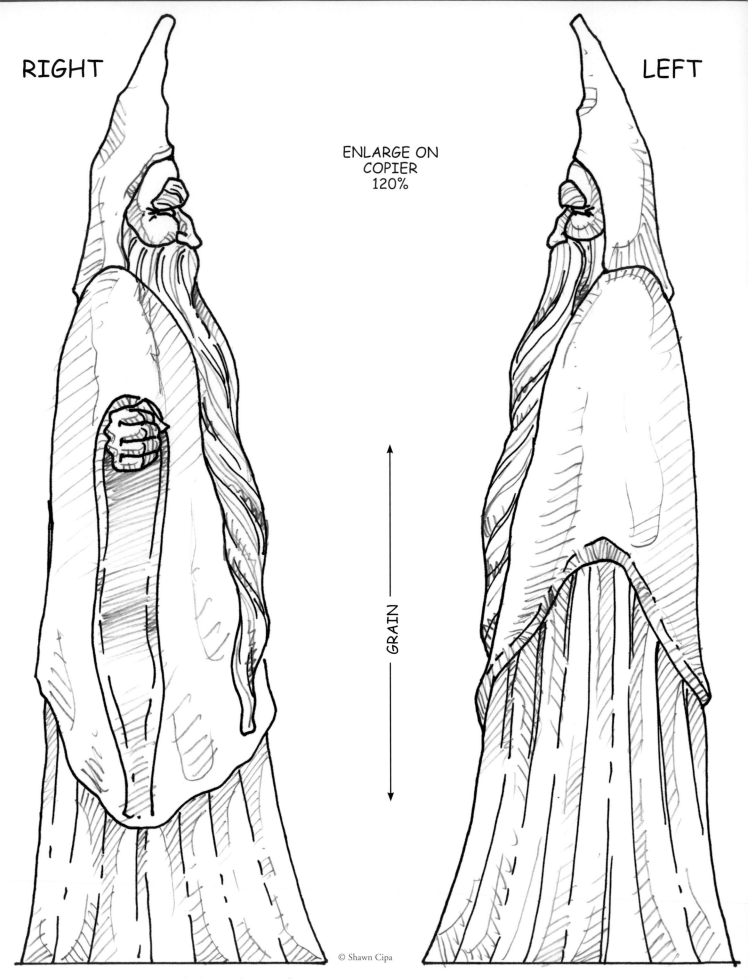

RIGHT

LEFT

ENLARGE ON
COPIER
120%

GRAIN

© Shawn Cipa

Materials List

- Basswood block 12" x 6" x 4"
- Walking staff, species of your choice
  10" x 1¼" x ½"
- Larger bladed rough-out knife
- Standard carving knife or pelican knife
- Detail knife
- Large #5 sweep 1¼" shallow gouge
- #12 sweep ½" V-tool
- #5 sweep ¾" fishtail gouge
- #5 sweep ½" fishtail gouge
- Small ¼" shallow gouge

- ½" half round gouge
- ⅜" veiner
- ³⁄₁₆" or ⅛" veiner
- ¹⁄₁₆" veiner (optional)
- Mallet
- Vise or clamping system of your choice
- 50/50 mixture of alcohol and water in a spray bottle
- Pencil or fine marker
- Band saw
- Hand drill and ¼" bit

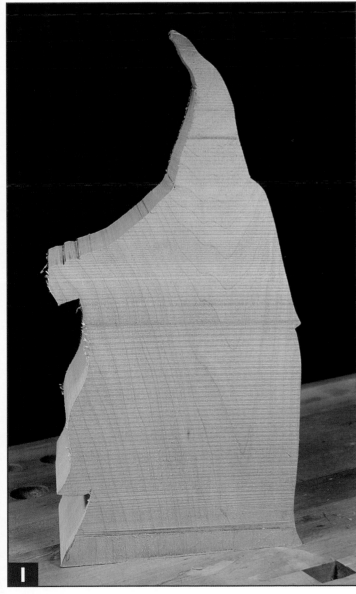

Front view of the band sawed blank.

Side view of the band sawed blank.

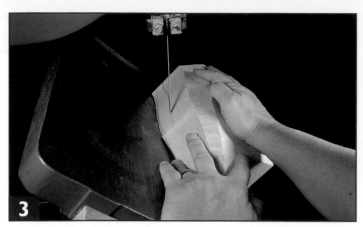

3

With the band saw table set at 45 degrees, trim off the front and back corners on the Wizard's left side. Do not cut on the right side of the Wizard, where his extended arm is.

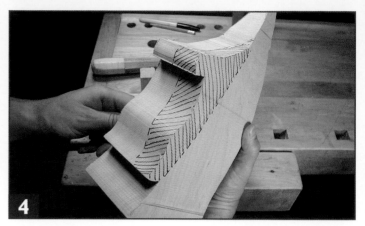

4

The first thing to do is to remove the excess wood in the extended arm area. A hollow must be created here. The drawn guidelines are merely approximate; liberty can be taken for removal of the waste wood.

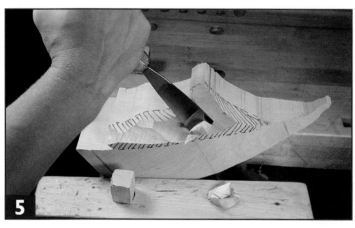

5

With the blank securely vised in, carve away the hard corner with a large shallow gouge. I'm using a 1¼" wide gouge with a #5 sweep. You can push by hand or use a mallet; because it is bulky work here, I prefer the mallet.

6

Notice how I have generously scalloped out this area to help expose the Wizard's arm.

7

With that cut completed, begin to round off the whole figure. Begin with the side that includes the extended arm. Smooth out the valley created from Step 5. I am using the same gouge here so far.

8

I have tapered the arm area, slightly, from the back, as shown.

9 Round out the other, "armless" side. A considerable amount of waste can be removed here. Be sure to smoothly taper the shape up to the head area. Start in the front…

10 …and move to the back. Taper all the way up to the tip of the hood.

11 After the left and right sides are rounded, taper out the whole back side. Starting from the bottom, work your way up.

12 Do the same for the front; however, leave a little extra where the beard will be—just left of center. The beard will follow the "ridge" created from the valley.

13 Progress so far: The front of the Wizard has been rounded and tapered back to form a ridge, indicated by the dotted line. Notice that the line is not centered but more to the left. The entire body is already taking shape.

14 The view from the side with the extended arm. Notice the tapers on the front and back. The taper is more pronounced on the front. Also notice that I have left the edge of the draping robe (under the fist) uncarved for now.

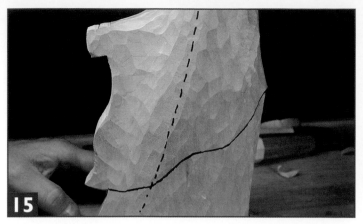

15 I have drawn a line to show the separation of the outer robe from the inner robe. Make them flow, as if the wind were blowing.

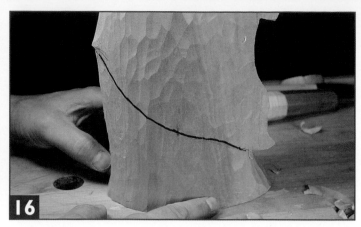

16 The line showing the separation of the outer robe and the inner robe continues to the back of the piece.

17 With the carving vised securely, use a #12 ½" V-tool and mallet to trench out the area below the outer robe line. Start in the front, and work your way all the way around the piece.

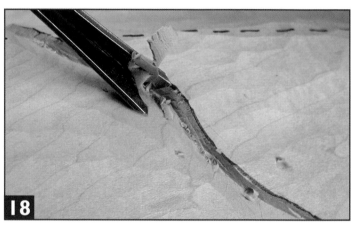

18 Detail: Be sure to tilt the V-tool toward the bottom when trenching, using the tool to plane out wood below the line. This helps to create the layering effect.

19 Once the line has been trenched out, take the ¼" gouge and taper the inner robe from the bottom up. Go all the way around. Keep the very bottom of the robe flared, gently scalloping inward as you move up.

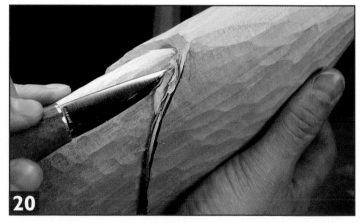

20 Using a large rough-out knife, go back and clean up the separation of the inner and outer robes—especially the high point on the Wizard's left side…

21

…and the low point on his right, under the outstretched arm.

22

Progress: Notice how the inner robe flares at the bottom, then neatly tapers up and appears to disappear behind the outer robe. There is clearly a suggestion of flowing movement here.

23

Using the rough-out knife, take a little time to shape the hood area. Round out the corners, but leave extra material for the face.

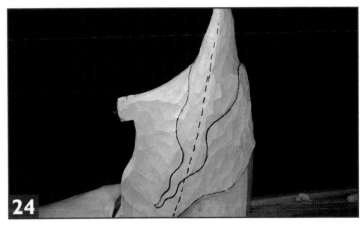

24

Draw in the outline of the beard and hood section. Form and carve the beard however you wish—slightly wavy or very curly. Remember that the wind will have the same effect on the beard as it has on the robes. The beard should flow off-center to the Wizard's right, just like the robes.

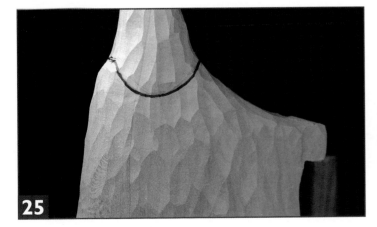

25

The line of the hood extends around the back side of the carving.

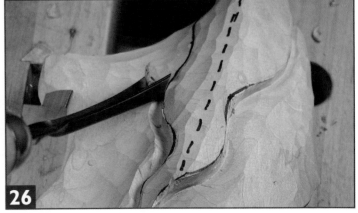

26

Vise the carving securely. Use the V-tool to define the beard and hood; tilt the tool on its side to help plane away waste. You may cut deeply around the beard, depending on how much excess you left along the centerline…

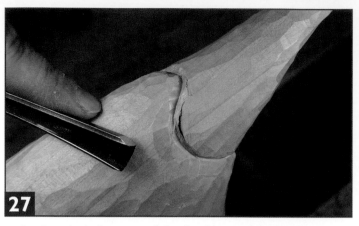

27

…but keep it shallow around the shoulders and the hood.

28

Now that the beard and hood area is well defined, it's time to cut back the excess on the outer hood. For this, I use a #5 ¾" fishtail gouge.

29

Thin out the back as well, scalloping upward from the edge of the robe.

30

The lower robe has a layered, pleated detail. Draw in vertical lines at random distances from each other. Be sure to make the lines bend with the flow of the figure. Make sure you are happy with the overall shape of the lower robe before moving forward!

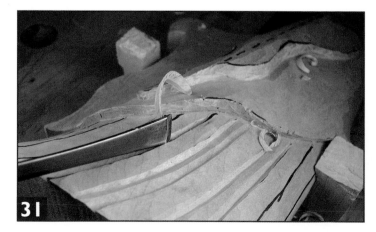

31

Vise in the carving again. Using the V-tool, apply the planing technique by tilting the tool on its side. (See Step 18.) This creates the effect of layering. Some pleats will appear to be deeper than others. For the best effect, keep it random.

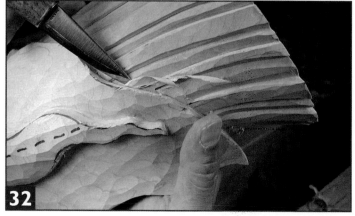

32

Using the rough-out knife, clean up the area where the pleats disappear up into the outer robe. Also, clean up your V-cuts and add a little more definition.

33

As a final touch, vertically scallop each pleat with a #5 ½" fishtail gouge. Use a ¼" shallow gouge for the more narrow folds. (Note: Both gouges are shown to illustrate the point.)

34

The completed effect.

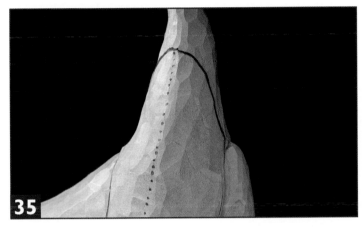

35

To begin the Wizard's face, we must first define the edge of his hood. Draw it in, as shown. Remember that the center of the face is turned to the left a bit, which offsets it from the true center of the body. I have redefined the centerline to illustrate this point.

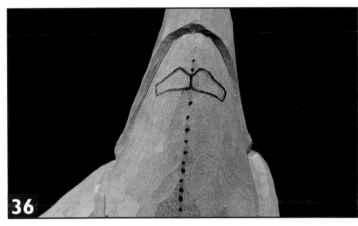

36

Using the V-tool and your knife of choice, separate the face from the hood, as shown. I prefer to use the pelican—it is good for turning cuts. Don't go too deep here, and let the shape of the beard flow right up into the sides of the face. Draw in the eyebrows.

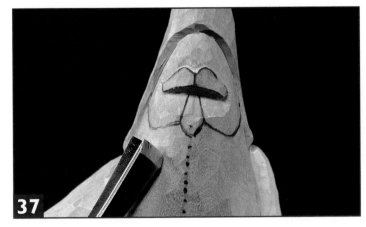

37

Using the V-tool, define the eyebrows by using the planing technique once again. You can use a smaller V-tool, but I still prefer to use the same larger one for this step. Draw in the nose and cheekbones, as shown.

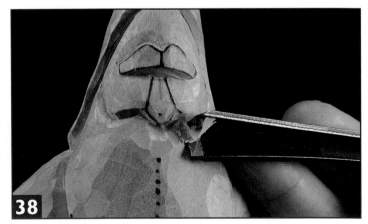

38

Still using the V-tool, separate the cheeks and nose ball from the mustache and beard section.

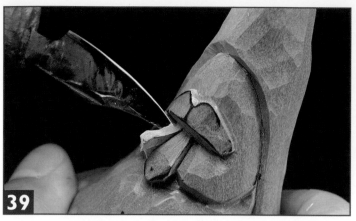

39

Using a detail knife (or whichever knife you prefer—I'm using my trusty pelican blade here), plunge straight into the face along each side of the nose. Then come back and remove a wedge on both sides to reveal the nose itself.

40

Progress: At this point, the profile should look some thing like this.

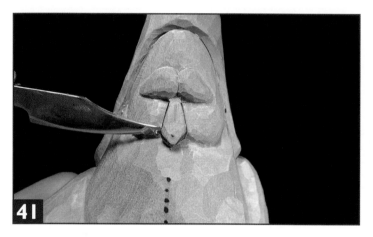

41

Using the detail or pelican knife, shape the cheeks by rounding the corners left by the V-tool. Notice how I have further defined the eyebrows by rounding and separating them at the center.

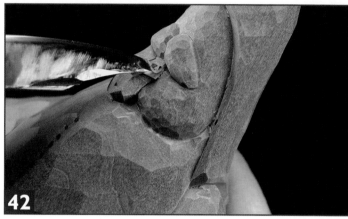

42

Shape the nose by scalloping each side. Starting at the nose ball, scallop out a small sliver upward toward the eyebrows. Don't cross over the centerline!

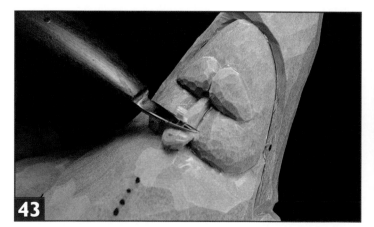

43

Shape the nose further by rounding out the nose ball. After that, switch to the detail knife and scallop out a small sliver right below the bridge of the nose. This forms a bony "bump."

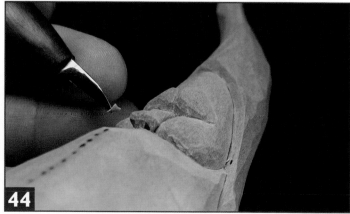

44

To complete the nose, carve out two tiny nostril holes underneath. Use the tip of the detail knife and a flick of the wrist.

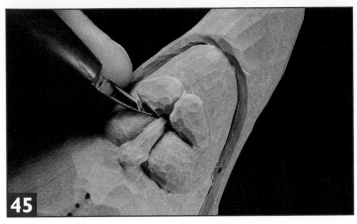

45 For the eyes, plunge deeply into the crease just below the eyebrow. Come back and carve out a tiny sliver horizontally, just enough to create a slit. This action creates a squinted eye.

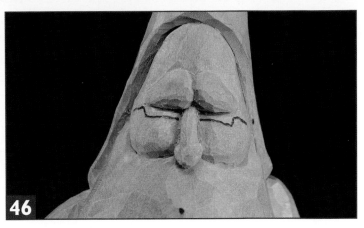

46 Draw in the sagging bags below the eyes, as shown.

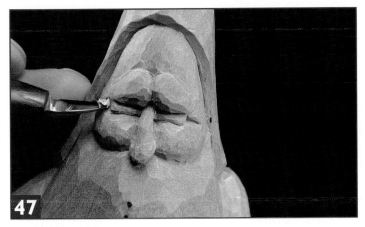

47 Plunge along the bag line with the detail knife. Come back and pare away small amounts below the plunge cut so that the bag is defined. Keep it shallow! As you do this, form the cheek into its final shape.

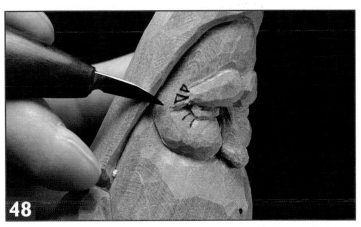

48 Final details of the eyes—crow's feet and wrinkles. Notice that I have drawn them in. Use the detail knife to chip cut these out.

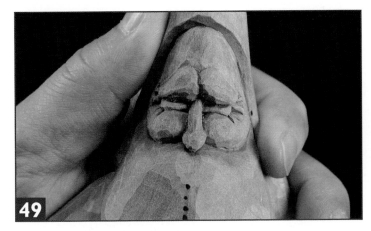

49 Progress: The face itself is complete. This is the time to clean up minute details or to make adjustments to the shape of the nose, the cheeks, or the eyebrows.

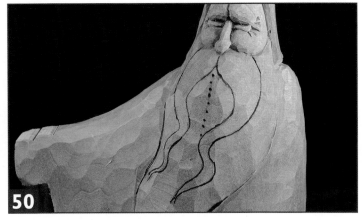

50 Draw in the mustache, as shown. Remember to keep it flowing with the direction of the beard.

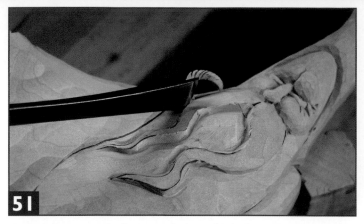

51

Define the mustache by using the V-tool. Tilt the tool and plane out the excess as you go. You can hold the carving by hand for this step, but it is easier and safer to vise the carving in. Be sure to leave a little extra wood for the lower lip.

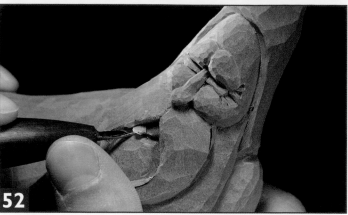

52

Using the detail knife, form the lower lip by making a series of plunge and chip cuts.

53

Use the knife to create a part in the mustache. At the same time, create an opening in the mouth by taking out a small chip.

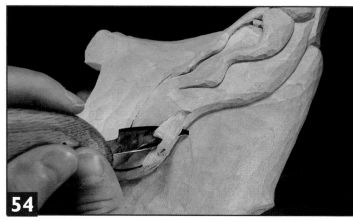

54

Before any texturing of the beard begins, we must first clean it up with the knife. Go back and round off any hard corners, redefine the V-cuts, and clean up the mustache and where it joins the face. I like to use the pelican knife; it's good for working bends and curves.

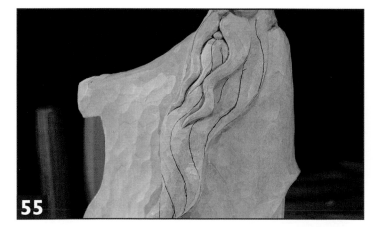

55

First draw in some light guidelines that will help to define the direction of the windblown beard. Notice how the lower, tapered part seems to twist around.

56

Following these guidelines (loosely), trench out some texture with a ³⁄₈" veiner. These cuts establish the "peaks and valleys" of the beard. I prefer to use the vise to hold the carving for this step.

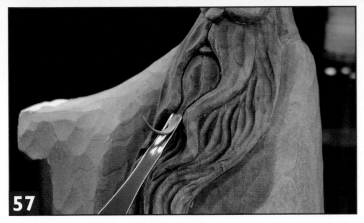

57

Now come back with a ³⁄₁₆" or ⅛" veiner. Texture the peaks and valleys, and remember to follow the flow. Spray the area lightly with a 50/50 alcohol–water mix. This helps the knife to cut smoothly through the constantly changing grain direction. Also texture the eye brows at this time.

58

If this is enough detail for you, stop here. I prefer to come back with an even smaller veiner and add a little more detail. I'm using a ¹⁄₁₆" veiner here.

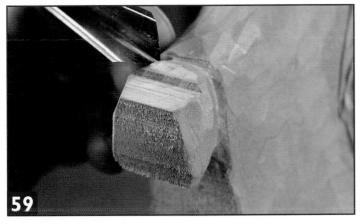

59

To begin the Wizard's right hand (it is assumed his left hand is hidden within the folds of his robe), separate it from the robe using the V-tool.

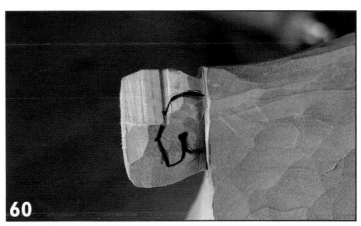

60

Before any shaping, a hole must first be drilled to accommodate the Wizard's staff. To do this, we must establish the placement of the thumb. Draw this in, on top as well as the front, as shown.

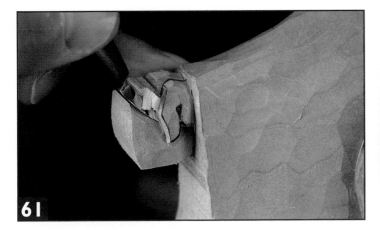

61

Using the detail knife, form the thumb by cutting back the surrounding material. Cut back enough to make the thumb about ⅛" thick.

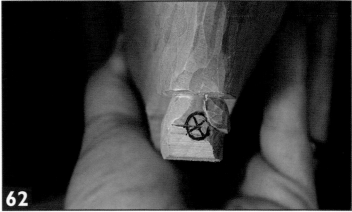

62

After the thumb is formed, we now know where to drill. Draw in a guideline, as shown. This will be a ¼" hole.

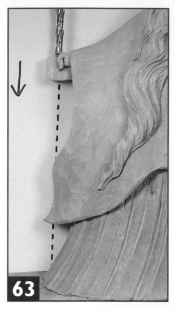

63

Using a ¼" bit, drill down from the top with a hand drill. It is important to line up the bit's path with the edge of the inner robe at the very bottom. You may have to angle outward a little. Take your time to get this right! If you are not comfortable using a hand drill for this step, you could bore a hole using the ¼" shallow gouge. If you accidentially mangle or break off a hand, do not fret! You can always fashion a new hand from a scrap of removed waste and glue it into place with yellow wood glue.

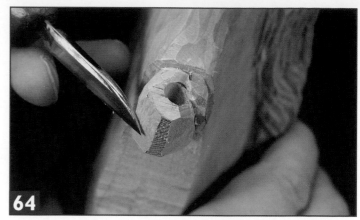

64

Next, shape the knuckles. Using the straight edged (sheepsfoot) knife, carefully knock off the front and back corners. Remember that the hole down through the center of the hand now makes the hand fragile!

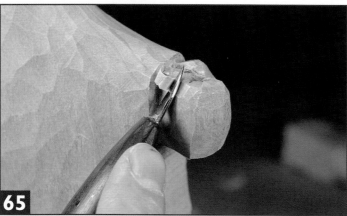

65

The shape of the fist is becoming apparent. At this point, *carefully* start rounding and shaping the fist. Do not remove too much wood. Look at your own fist and notice the angles.

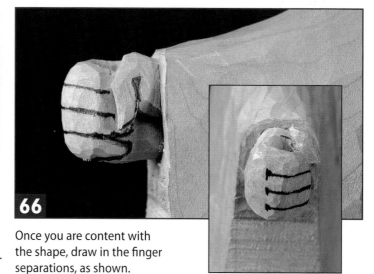

66

Once you are content with the shape, draw in the finger separations, as shown.

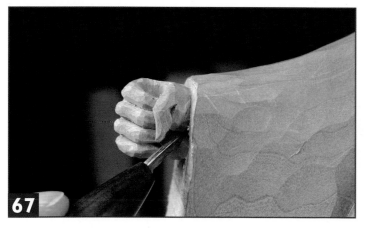

67

Using the detail knife, separate the fingers, rounding them as you go. Shape the thumb. Add creases where appropriate. Hollow the area underneath the thumb.

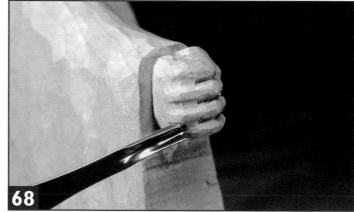

68

As a final touch, carve in the natural hollows between the knuckles with the ⅛" veiner.

Using the ⅜" veiner, hollow out the long, draping sleeve area. With the detail or pelican knife, clean up the area where the fist protrudes.

Add some wind movement to the outer robe. Draw in some loose guidelines and use a ½" half-round gouge. To create some shallow valleys, use the ½" fishtail to smooth out some areas. This is very free form, so use your artistic license.

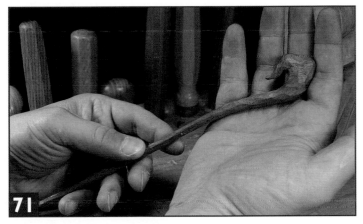

Prepare a wizard's staff out of the wood of your choice. I cut a blank from black walnut and shaped it with a knife. Make sure the shaft is whittled down to a ¼" diameter where it will sit in the fist.

Fit the staff into the fist. Notch out a small area where the stick can fit into the edge of the robe, as shown. When you are satisfied with the fit, glue the staff into place with yellow wood glue.

Make sure the carving is clean and dust-free. Then the Wizard is complete and ready for finishing!

Materials List

- ¾" flat brush for large areas
- ¼" flat brush for smaller areas
- ¼" round brush for smaller areas
- ⅛" round brush for details
- Boiled linseed oil thinned with mineral spirits
- Spray can of fast-drying clear matte enamel or brush-on Deft lacquer
- Brown gel wood stain
- Yellow wood glue
- Disposable stain brushes
- Cotton rags
- Latex gloves

Colors

- Slate blue
- Midnight blue
- Light gray
- Lavender
- Deep purple
- Antique white
- Deep yellow
- Beige
- Pure white
- Maroon
- Pale gold

Before beginning, go back and review the painting and finishing section in the "Getting Started" chapter, pages 8 and 9.

1 Using a disposable stain brush, apply a light coat of thinned boiled linseed oil to the entire carving. Be sure to get it in all crevices. This will seal the wood and allow the paint to flow and blend more smoothly. It also gives the wood a nice amber patina prior to applying washes of color.

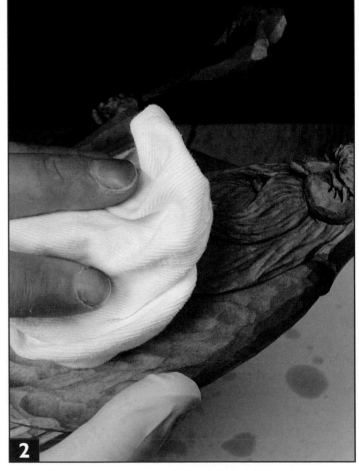

2 Wipe off the excess oil with a clean cotton rag. Let the carving sit overnight, or at least for several hours. (It helps to wear at least one glove when handling the carving. The linseed oil will absorb into your skin and make your hands smell even after washing.) Be sure to dispose of oily rags properly.

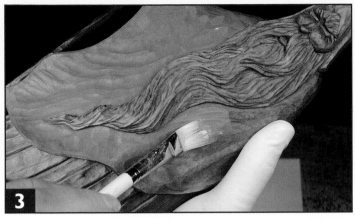

3 We will first paint the Wizard's outer robe and hood. Referring to the Painting and Finishing section, apply a wash coat of slate blue with a large ¾" flat brush.

4 Don't forget the edges of the robe.

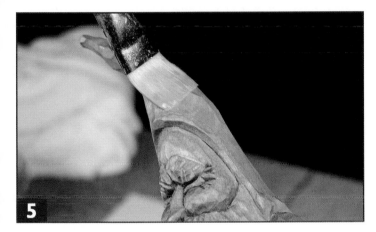

5 Paint the hood the same color.

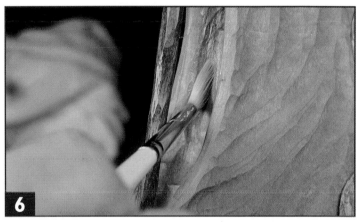

6 Use a ¼" round brush to get into the inner sleeve. Don't get any paint on the walking staff.

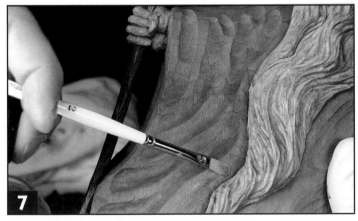

7 Using a ¼" flat brush, apply a wash of midnight blue sparingly to the pockets and folds of the robe. Also apply it around the beard and hood. Blend it into the slate blue; add a little water where needed. This layering helps to create more depth.

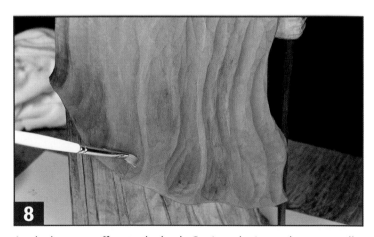

8 Apply the same effect to the back. Get into the inner sleeve as well.

9 To start the inner robe, paint every other pleat with a wash of light gray. Use the ¼" flat brush.

10 Paint the remaining pleats with lavender.

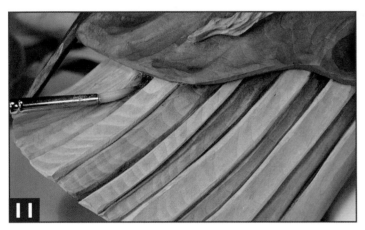

11 Using the ¼" round brush, layer a thin wash of deep purple over the lavender pleats; apply it into the crevices and up near the outer robe. Blend it into the lavender.

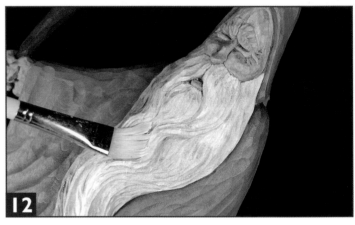

12 Now for the beard. Using the ¾" flat brush, apply a wash coat of antique white with a touch of deep yellow mixed in. Be very careful not to touch the Wizard's face with the brush. Use a smaller brush, such as the ¾" flat or round ones, if you must when painting close to the face.

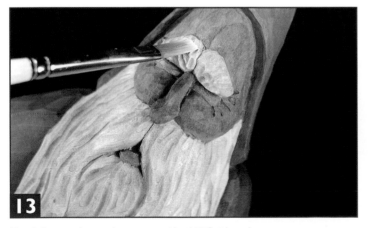

13 Don't forget the eyebrows; use the ¼" flat brush.

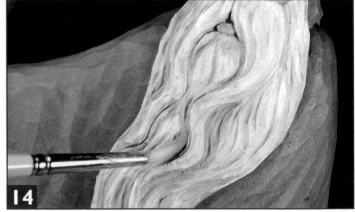

14 Using the ¼" round brush, create "low-lights" in the beard by applying thin coats of beige into the valleys and edges and around the lower lip, under the mustache. This layering technique must be used sparingly to be effective. Be sure to blend it into the antique white.

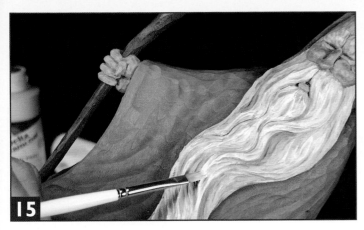

15

Apply the final layer to finish the beard, mustache, and eyebrows. Using the ¼" flat brush, sparingly apply pure white highlights by lightly scraping across the peaks of texture. Thin the white a bit, but not as much as the other colors.

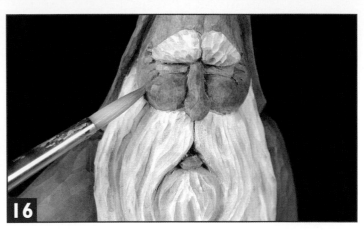

16

The face and hand do not need to be painted; the application of oil gave the basswood a nice tanned flesh tone. However, I do like to add a little color to the cheeks. Using the ¼" round brush, apply a very thin dab of maroon wash to the cheeks. Blend it in.

17

Add some decoration to the outer robe. Using a ⅛" round detail brush, apply tiny specks of full-strength pale gold in random patterns, as though they were stars in a night sky. If you are ambitious, you could even add constellations! Let the carving dry for at least an hour.

18

Seal the carving prior to antiquing. Here I am spraying on a few light coats of fast-drying, clear, matte enamel. It must be matte; the last thing we want is a glossy carving! Let the carving dry overnight.

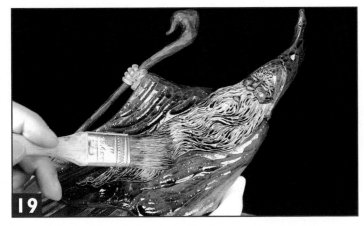

19

Using a disposable stain brush, apply a brown gel wood stain. Slather it on, working it into the nooks.

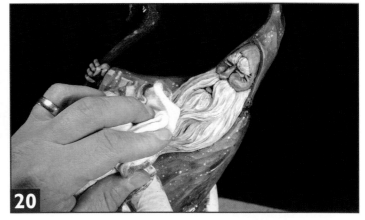

20

Immediately wipe off the excess with a clean cotton rag. Let the carving dry overnight before handling it. Your Wizard is complete!

The Dragon

Dragons take a leading role in mythology in almost every known culture. It is no wonder then that they have a permanent position as an icon of the fantastic. From the beginning of recorded history to as recent as 400 years ago, the existence of dragons was thought to be commonplace, and recorded sightings were plentiful. "Zoologically extinct," dragons now only exist in our imagination.

There are many different types of dragons; I have chosen a wyvern for this project. A wyvern is a variation of the common dragon, possessing only two limbs and sporting a serpent-like body. Wyverns were often portrayed in heraldry and were considered aggressive and predatory.

This fellow is an excellent study of form and is great practice for carving with constantly changing grain directions. This design will prepare you for some of the other more involved projects in this book.

When band sawing the blank, take great care in the deep areas. Take out small bites, and work your way in. Although the shape is involved, the stock is only two inches thick and should cut easily. The provided front and back view patterns are for reference only—you will be cutting the blank from the side view only. The block before sawing will need to measure 10" x 6" x 2". This project would also be excellent as a much larger carving with more details added.

Roughing out the carving will require the piece to be held in a vise; finer details can be done with the carving held in your hand, but mind the delicate areas such as the tongue, beard, and tail.

This is a fun one. Take your time and carefully read the steps and study the photographs as you go.

RIGHT
SIDE

GRAIN

© Shawn Cipa

LEFT
SIDE

GRAIN

© Shawn Cipa

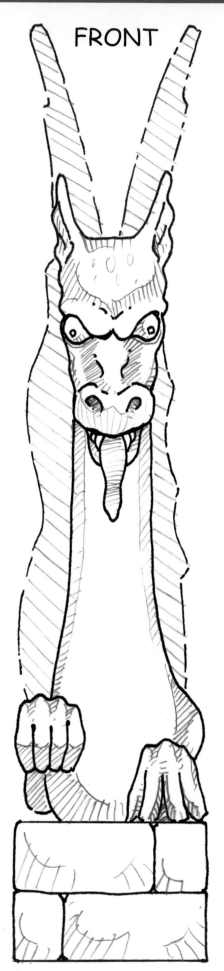

FRONT

GRAIN

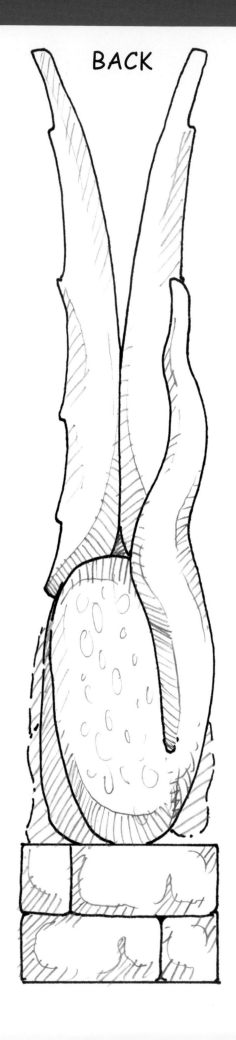

BACK

© Shawn Cipa

Materials List

- Basswood block 10" x 6" x 2"
- Larger bladed rough-out knife
- Standard (sheepsfoot) carving knife, or (I prefer) a pelican knife
- Detail knife
- Large #5 sweep 1¼" shallow gouge
- #12 sweep ½" V-tool
- ⅛" V-tool
- #5 sweep ¾" fishtail gouge
- #5 sweep ½" fishtail gouge
- Small ¼" shallow gouge
- ½" half round gouge
- ⅜" veiner
- ⅛" veiner
- ¹⁄₁₆" veiner
- Mallet
- Pull saw (optional)
- Vise or clamping system of your choice
- 50/50 mixture of alcohol and water in a spray bottle
- Pencil or fine marker
- Band saw
- Scroll saw or coping saw (optional)
- Drill press or hand drill with ⅜" bit

A side view of the band sawed blank. Two ⅜" holes have been drilled: one for the void created by the Dragon's looping body and one for the void between his underbelly and the base. I used a drill press for this, but a hand drill will work just as well. The space between the Dragon's beard and his lolling tongue has been left unresolved for now. The delicate parts could break during the rough-out stage.

The blank on edge. Find the center by measuring; then mark a centerline from the front all the way to the back. As excess wood is removed, this will be a reference to help you keep things in proportion.

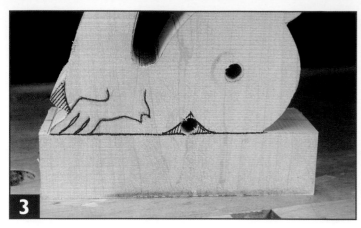

3

Referring to the pattern, draw in the top surface of the base and the left foot. The feet will be the outermost projections on each side, so they must be defined first.

4

Draw in the top of the base and the right foot on the other side, as shown.

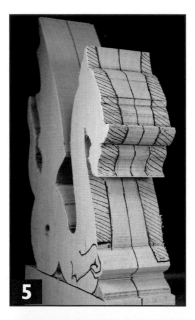

5

Draw guidelines in the front for roughing out. The top (his ears) should be about ¾" out from the centerline on each side. Taper it down to about ½" from the centerline at his muzzle, and begin to flare back out to ¾" from the centerline again, right above the feet.

6

We'll start on the Dragon's left side. His foot will be most prominent, so leave it intact and remove the wood around it. We'll leave the base intact as well. Vise the piece in securely. I start by separating the base and the foot from the body with the #12 ½" V-tool and the mallet.

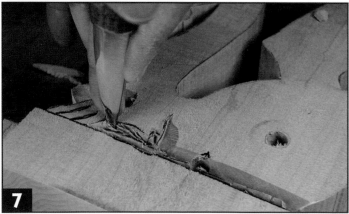

7

Now that the separation is established, further the progress by plunge cutting straight in along the V-cuts. I'm using my rough-out knife here.

8

Using a combination of the rough-out knife, the #5 ½" fishtail gouge, and the ¼" shallow gouge, continue to remove excess wood from the Dragon's underbelly. Use the knife to keep plunging deeper; remove wood with the fishtail gouge.

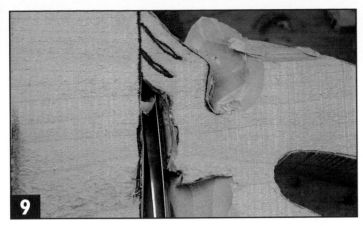

Use the ¼" shallow gouge to get into the tight area between the leg and the base. The knife's point can help to clean up the inner corners. Clear out excess wood above the foot as well.

Once this is accomplished, we can remove the excess wood up the neck and around the head. Be sure to carefully follow the guide lines we drew in Step 5. Use the large #5 1¼" gouge and mallet. Keep the sides on a flat plane; do not round the neck or head yet.

Progress: Notice that I have removed the waste up to the guideline. Also, notice how I have left the foot intact but scalloped in around it to form the neck and shoulders.

The right side of the Dragon is accomplished in the same manner, even though the right leg is in a different position. Repeat Steps 6 through 11. Don't round corners yet; it's easier to visualize the cuts when the basic shapes are blocked out first.

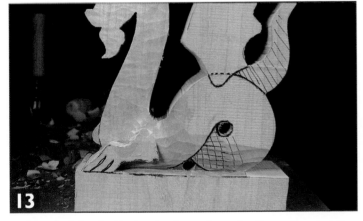

Back to the left side. Notice the drawn lines; the Dragon's serpentine body twists under itself, like a donut. (Study the picture of the finished piece.) The tail emerges out the other side. The next step is to cut back the shaded areas.

With the piece vised in securely, start at the inner twist. As before, plunge straight in with the rough-out knife along the drawn line. Remove excess wood with the ½" fishtail gouge. Repeat this process until you have dug in about halfway through (equal to the centerline) at the deepest point. Taper the lower half of the circle into the plunged area as you go.

15

Now remove the excess wood from the tail. Once again, plunge cut with the knife and remove waste with the ½" fishtail gouge. Block out the tail all the way to the centerline, as shown.

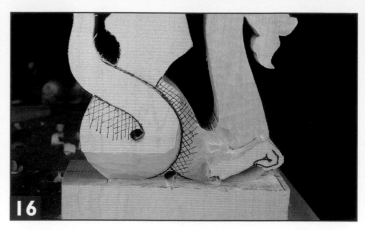

16

Now the right side. Notice the drawn line. The back half and tail of the Dragon are dominant on this side. The next step is to cut back the shaded areas.

17

Vise the piece in again. First, work on the area disappearing under the tail. Remove the waste in the same manner as the previous steps, going only about ½" deep at the stop cut. As before, taper the circle into the plunged area.

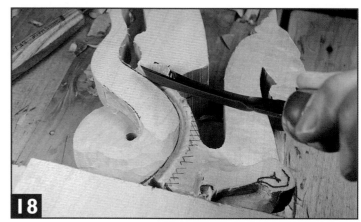

18

Next, remove waste from the area of the upper body that is partially obscured by the escalating tail. Using the ½" V-tool and mallet, establish the division…

19

…and continue by removing more excess with the ½" fishtail gouge and rough-out knife combined. Don't go any deeper than ½". Remove only the wing portion that is closest to the tail, as shown.

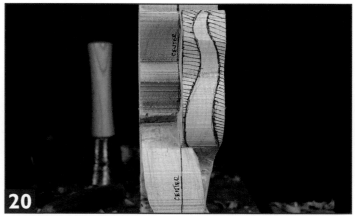

20

Notice the "tilt" we have created on the lower portion of the Dragon's body. Draw in the wavy shape of the tail, as shown.

21

With the carving vised in, proceed to remove the waste around both sides of the tail with the ½" fishtail gouge.

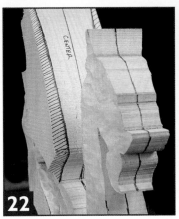
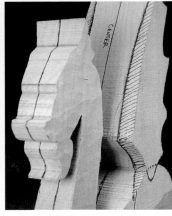

22

Draw in lines for waste removal of the wings. Shown are left and right versions of the Dragon's front. Notice that the contour starts at the tips, curves slightly inward to the "elbow" joints, and flares back out a bit where the wing joins the body.

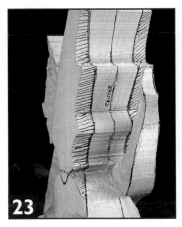

23

The rear view of the wing contours. The contours follow the same path as those we marked on the front of the Dragon.

24

Vise the carving in. Using the 1¼" gouge, remove the excess wood from each side of the outer wings, following the established guidelines from Steps 22 and 23. Notice that the guidelines on the Dragon's left side will "eat" into the body a bit where the wing is attached.

25

Notice the contour of the wings' outer shape. Draw in guidelines for waste removal between the wings, as shown.

26

You may remove this waste with a rough-out knife or ½" half round gouge, but I prefer to use a pull saw (refer to the Tools section). When using the saw, be careful not to mar the back of the Dragon's head or the tip of the tail. Have the carving vised in an upright position for this step.

27

Progress: A rear view of the results.

28

Using the rough-out knife, separate the wings from each other. Starting in the front center, slice out pieces little by little, all the while maintaining the center groove. Do not fight the grain direction. Vice the carving at an angle that is comfortable to you.

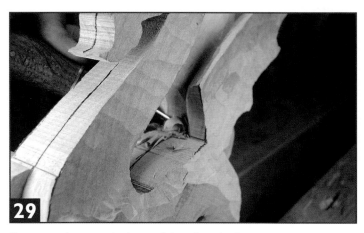

29

Carve out down to the base of the wings in the same manner, as shown.

30

Using the rough-out knife, remove waste from the backs of the wings. Use the same technique as in the front. This proves to be more difficult because the tail is partially in the way. Take your time and cut out small bites. Don't break all the way through.

31

Progress: The inside of the wings is completed—a rear view. They are still connected in the middle but are tapered to the edges to give the illusion of being thin. You may find that the ½" fishtail gouge will help in the final shaping.

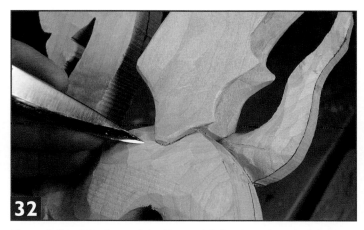

32

I have defined the base of the Dragon's left wing where it attaches to the body. Use the V-tool, and clean the area up with the rough-out knife. On the right side, this area is obscured by the Dragon's twisting tail.

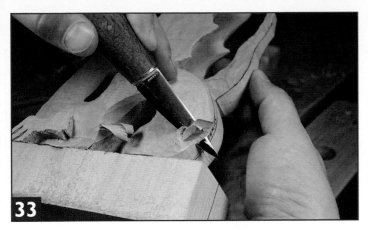

33 Now to round the body into shape. Using the rough-out knife, carve away the hard corners. Beware of the ever-changing grain direction. Work on rounding the Dragon's left side first.

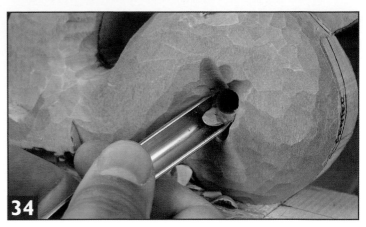

34 Use the ⅜" veiner to round out the inner corners, such as those on the twist (as shown) and at the inner base of the neck.

35 I like to use my pelican knife to fine-tune the shape and surface of the area. The shape of the blade makes it easy to work into the many curves. A standard carving knife will work, of course, but any knife with a curved cutting edge is ideal for this carving in particular.

36 Now shape the Dragon's right side, including his tail. Use the same tools and techniques.

37 Progress: The Dragon's lower body has its final shape. Notice the tapered tail and how it overlaps and partially obscures the base of the wing.

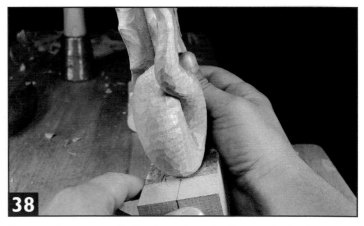

38 Progress: A rear view. Notice how the tail rolls over the body.

To complete the wings, we must first scallop out the surface. For this, I use the # 5 ¾" fishtail gouge. Leave the main spine of the wing intact and work toward the tips.

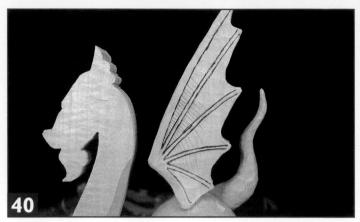

Draw in the bony structures (known as fingers) of the wing, extending from the lower joint out to each tip. Refer to the pattern for exact placement.

Finally, hollow out the membrane between each bony finger. For the tightest areas, use ¹⁄₁₆" and ⅛" veiners (shown at left). Use the ¼" shallow gouge for the remaining areas. By removing wood from between the lines, the fingers are created.

Complete the other side, as shown.

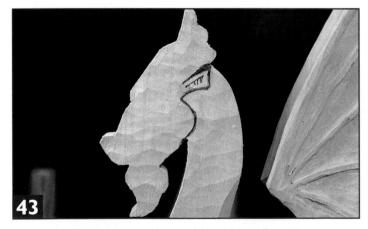

Draw in lines that separate the head from the neck, as shown. Refer to the pattern to get the correct shape. This step outlines the Dragon's head crest, ears, and jaw line. Draw in both sides.

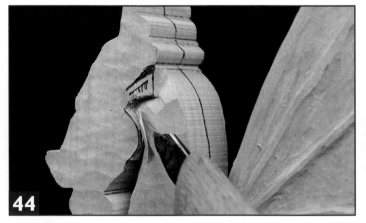

Using the knife of your choice (I'm using the pelican), create stop cuts along these lines and begin to cut back some excess wood behind the head, as shown.

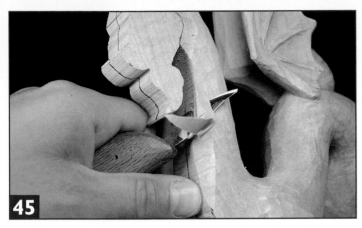

45

With the head now isolated, we can begin to shape the neck. Using your knife, carve down all of the hard corners and round the neck to a graceful curve. Use your centerline as a reference in order to keep each side in balance.

46

Progress: The neck is complete and blended into the rest of the body.

47

A front view of the chest. Notice how I have rounded the area underneath the raised right foot. The areas to be removed—about ⅜" from the center on each side—are marked with diagonal lines.

48

Use your knife to carve away the excess. Smooth out the surface of the chest as it is exposed.

49

Using the knife, carve off the corners of the Dragon's left foot, as shown.

50

Shape the foot by scalloping from the tip upward.

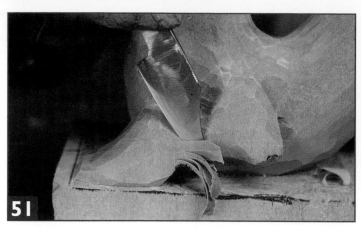

51

Shape the rest of the leg by rounding any hard edges. Refer to the photos of the finished piece to help you in the shaping process.

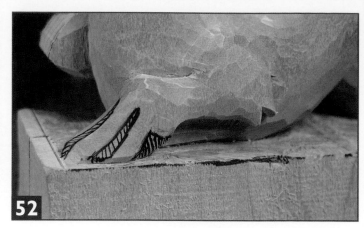

52

Draw in the "voids" to be removed that will, in turn, create the individual toes, as shown. There will be four toes total.

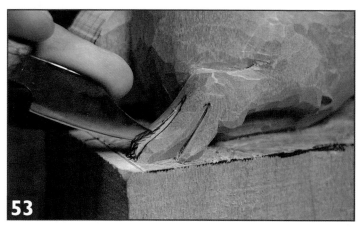

53

Using your detail or pelican knife, carefully carve out each void. Round and shape the toes as you go.

54

A front view of the completed left foot. I have scalloped out small indentations between the tops of the toes to form the knuckles.

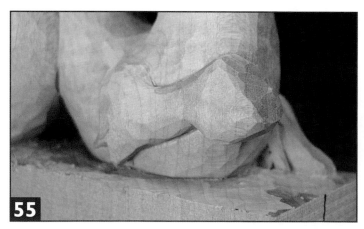

55

Fashion the right foot in much the same way. Round and shape the leg and fist…

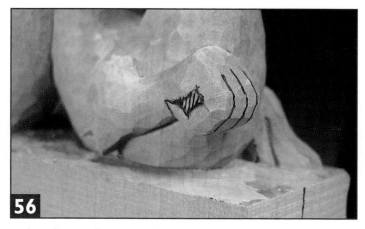

56

…then draw in the toes, as shown…

57 …and carve to define. Shown is the completed right foot, clenched into a fist. Notice the pointed outer claw and the indentations between the knuckles.

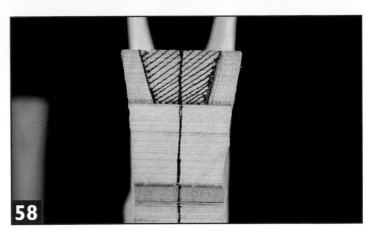

58 Draw in the area to be removed between the head crests, as shown.

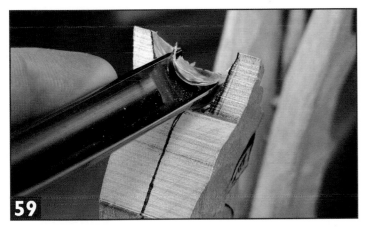

59 Remove the void with a ½" half-round gouge. Take care not to carve below the forehead line.

60 Approach the area from behind. Because the wings are in the way, you will have to attack from the sides. The idea is to have the slope of the neck follow right up to the top of the Dragon's head.

61 Start to shape the Dragon's head with the knife. Again, I prefer to use my pelican blade here; it allows me to carve into curves and is helpful for scalloping and hollowing. Start by carving off the hard corners.

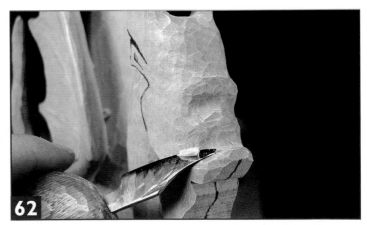

62 Shape the profile. Smooth out the forehead and snout. Form a "hump" around the brow. Leave sufficient material for the bulging eyeballs. It may help to refer closely to the photos of the finished carving while executing this step.

63

Thin out the jaw area a little on each side to make it narrower than the forehead. At the same time, taper the beard and tongue section into a much thinner projection.

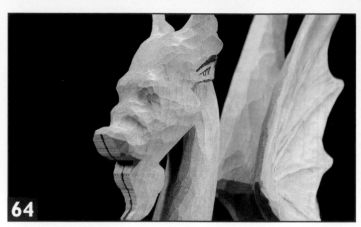

64

Progress: The facial structure is defined; notice the bony brow, the humped bridge, and the upturned snout. The forehead is slightly hollowed behind the brow and slopes upward. The jaws are narrowed, and the tongue/beard projection is tapered down.

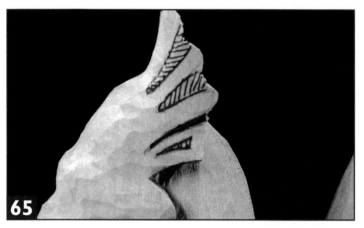

65

It's now time to detail the head crests. Notice the division of the crest and the lower ear. The shaded upper areas are to be scalloped out with the ⅛" veiner. The detail knife will perform the division of ear and crest, as well as hollow the ear with a chip cut.

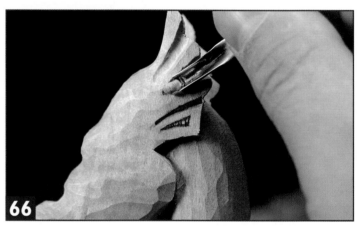

66

Scallop the crest to create a webbed look. As noted, I am using the ⅛" veiner. (The triangular area at the bottom of the crest is the ear.)

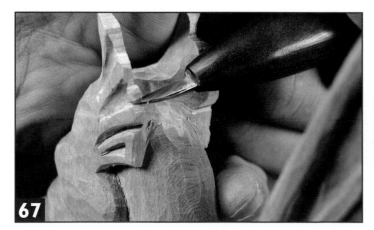

67

Notice that the ear has been separated from the crest by using the detail knife, and it has also been hollowed by removing a chip cut. Use the detail knife to clean up the back edges of the head crests. Do both sides.

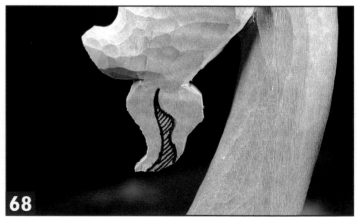

68

Referring to the pattern, draw in the void that separates the tongue from the beard. I perform the removal carefully with the band saw. You may remove it by hand with a detail knife, but you run the risk of snapping off the individual pieces. A scroll saw would also work nicely, or even a coping saw.

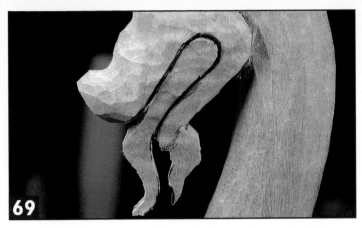

69

The wood has been removed. Draw in the mouth opening. Refer to the pattern for exact placement. Draw in both sides.

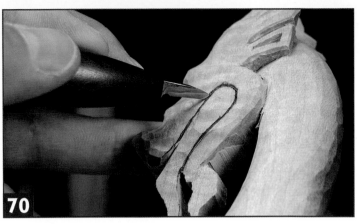

70

Using the detail knife, plunge cleanly and directly inward along the mouth lines. Do both sides.

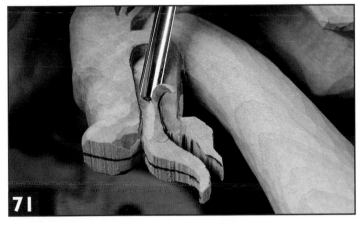

71

Using the ¼" shallow gouge and the detail knife, hollow out the mouth area. Incise deeper with the knife, if you must. Go ⅛" to ³⁄₁₆" deep.

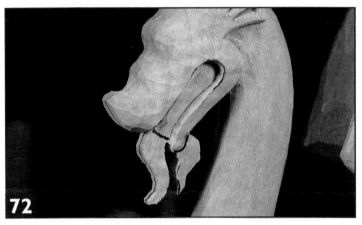

72

We now have a surface on which to carve the Dragon's teeth. Notice the two small lines I drew to separate the tongue from the teeth and the beard from the chin.

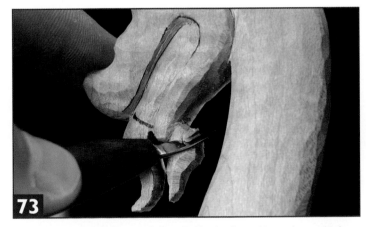

73

Using the detail knife, carefully whittle the beard into shape. Make it stand out from the chin, as shown. While you're at it, smooth out the saw marks under the jaws with the knife.

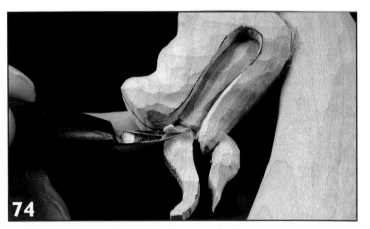

74

Notice the beard is complete. Using the detail knife, separate the tongue from the teeth by creating a stop cut along the guideline. Cut back the wood to thin out the tongue a bit. Carefully whittle the tongue into shape.

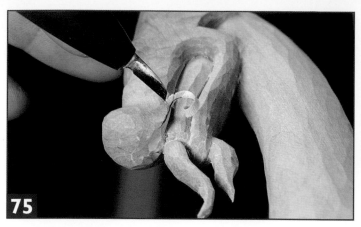

75

Using the detail knife, round the hard edge of the Dragon's lips. Go all the way around, upper and lower, and smooth out the Dragon's snout.

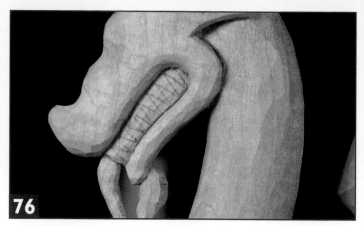

76

After the lips are rounded, draw the teeth in a zigzag fashion, as shown. Do it lightly in pencil, as I have done; marker lines will be too hard to erase with such small areas to carve.

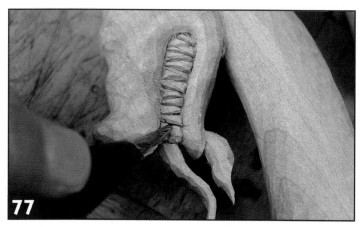

77

Using the point of the detail knife, incise tiny V-cuts along each line. Don't worry about perfect spacing; unevenness will only contribute to the Dragon's "snaggletooth" look. Carve both sides.

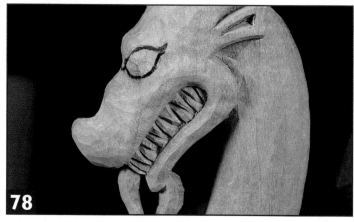

78

Scary teeth! Now he really looks like a dragon. Referring closely to the pattern, draw in the eyes. Be sure to position them over the hump we created earlier.

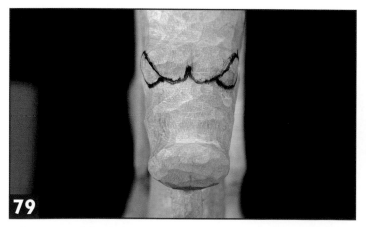

79

A front view of the drawn eyes. Notice the W-shaped brow line. Make sure you draw each eye in correct proportion to the other.

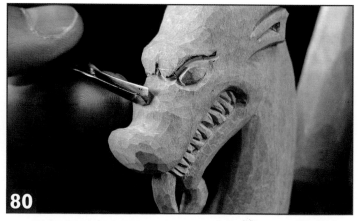

80

The easiest way to carve the eyes is to first trace all the lines with a ⅛" V-tool, as shown. This creates a starting point for the knife work.

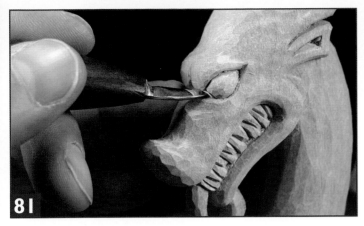

81

Using the detail knife, incise along all the V-cuts. Begin to round the eyeballs. At the same time, work the brow line into shape. Cut away from the bridge below the eyes, as you need to, in order to make the brow stand out more.

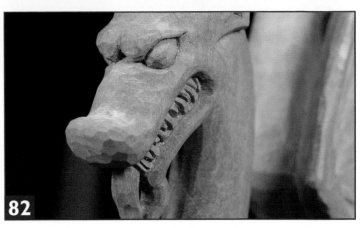

82

The eyes are completed. Notice the deep undercutting at the center of the brow. The eyes are rounded and appear to bulge out from the surface. The eyelids appear to be overlapping the eyeballs.

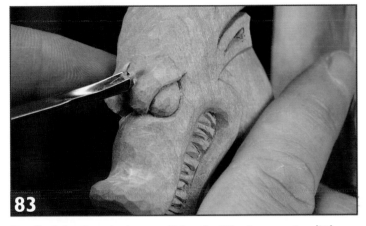

83

One final detail on the brow… Using the 1/8" veiner, create a little more definition by outlining the upper brow, as shown. Come back with the detail knife to smooth the cut out into the forehead, if need be.

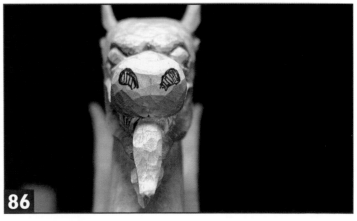

84

To further define the lips, use the 1/8" veiner. Starting at the side of the snout, trench out a groove along the contour of the mouth opening, as shown. Finish up at the turn at the back of the mouth. Do both sides.

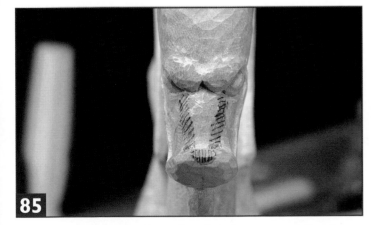

85

Notice the shaded areas. Using the 1/4" shallow gouge, define the bony bridge. Also, carve out a divot in the top of the snout (also shown as a shaded area) with the detail knife.

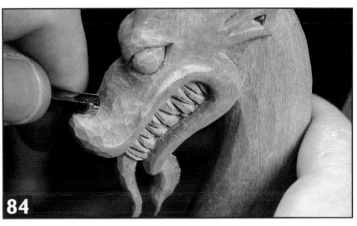

86

Draw in the nostril holes, as shown.

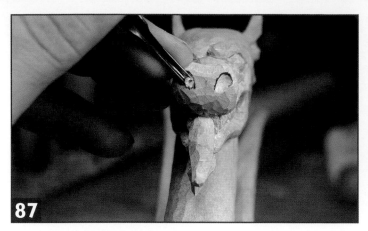

87

Carve the nostril holes with a 1/16" veiner.

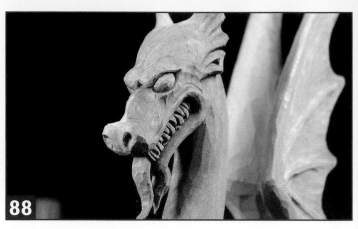

88

Progress: The head is complete.

89

Because the top surface of the base is end-grain, it may be difficult to carve smoothly. Spray the base with a 50/50 alcohol and water mixture (refer to the Alcohol and Water section on page 7). Vise the carving in an upright position.

90

Resurface the top of the base with the ½" fishtail gouge. Spray the wood as needed, and be careful not to mar the Dragon. Use the pelican or standard knife to clean up other areas where the Dragon makes contact with the base.

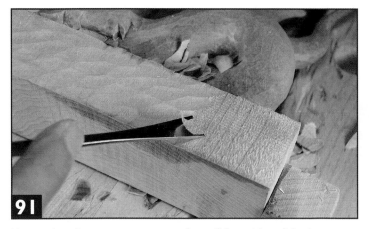

91

Next, using the same gouge, resurface all four sides of the base. It is preferable to leave a moderately textured surface.

92

The base will have the look of an old, rough-hewn stone wall. Draw in two layers of offset bricks, as shown. This does not have to be perfectly symmetrical—the rougher, the better.

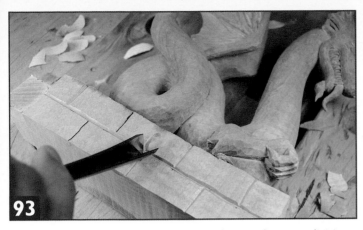

93

Using the ½" V-tool, trace all of your lines by trenching out divisions.

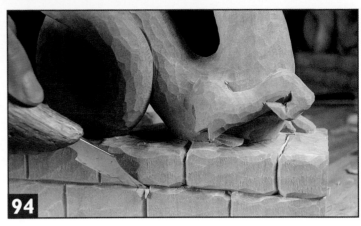

94

Using either the standard or the pelican knife, retrace each V-cut and deepen the seams between each stone. Round each intersection and corner. Make each stone look worn and uneven. Don't forget the top surface.

95

Make sure the carving is clean and dust-free. Your Dragon is complete and ready for finishing!

Materials List

- ¾" flat brush for large areas
- ¼" flat brush for smaller areas
- ¼" round brush for smaller areas
- ⅛" round brush for details
- Boiled linseed oil thinned with mineral spirits
- Spray can of fast-drying clear matte enamel or brush-on Deft lacquer
- Brown gel wood stain
- Disposable stain brushes
- Cotton rags
- Latex gloves

Colors

- Antique white
- Sage green
- Dark green
- Olive green
- Bright yellow
- Cinnamon
- Bright red
- Pure white
- Mauve
- Medium purple
- Mint green
- Light gray
- Black

1 Using a disposable stain brush, apply a light coat of thinned boiled linseed oil to the entire carving. Be sure to get it into all crevices. This will seal the wood and allow the paint to flow and blend more smoothly. It also gives the wood a nice amber patina.

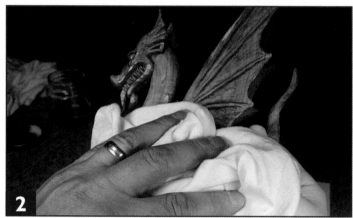

2 Wipe off the excess oil with a clean cotton rag. Let the carving sit overnight. (Wear at least one glove when handling the carving. The oil will absorb into your skin and make your hands smell even after washing.) Dispose of oily rags properly.

3 We will first paint the Dragon's chest and belly areas. Using a ¼" flat brush, apply a wash coat of antique white to the chest, as shown. Do not leave a hard edge where the paint stops; blend it into the wood.

4 Progress: Notice how the antique white is applied all the way up the neck under the chin. Also notice the blended edge of color.

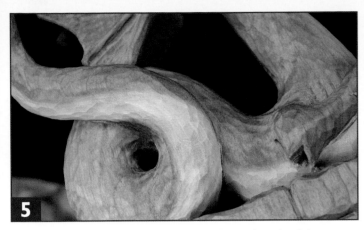

5

Continue painting the antique white on the underside of the Dragon. This photo shows the right side view of the painted belly. Placement is important; it helps to suggest the twisting of the snakelike body.

6

Taper the antique white paint to match the taper of the tail.

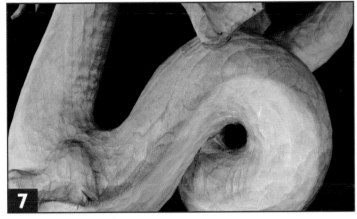

7

A left side view of the painted belly. Refer closely to the photos of the finished piece for placement of the color.

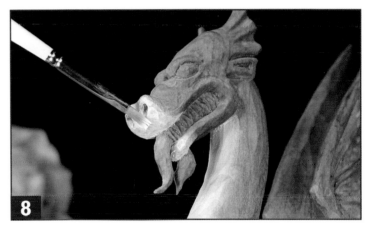

8

Using the same brush, apply some antique white to the front of the snout and chin, as shown.

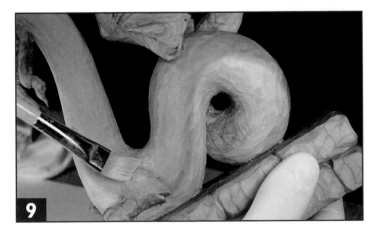

9

Using a ¾" flat brush, apply a wash coat of sage green to the entire body (not the wings). Be sure to blend the edges into the antique white.

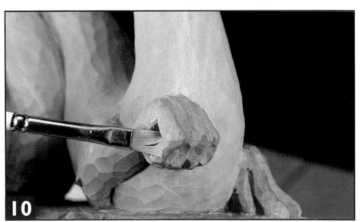

10

Using the ¼" flat brush, paint both feet sage green.

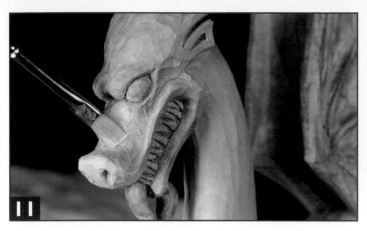

11

With the same brush, carefully paint the face sage green. Avoid getting paint on the eyeballs and teeth. Blend the sage green into the antique white areas.

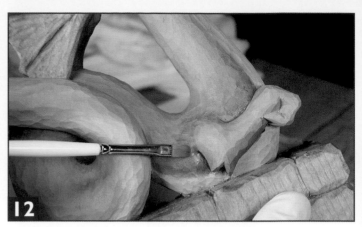

12

Using the ¼" flat brush, apply a wash of dark green as a shadowing effect over the sage green. Apply it around the feet and along the edges of the antique white areas. Shown is the right side.

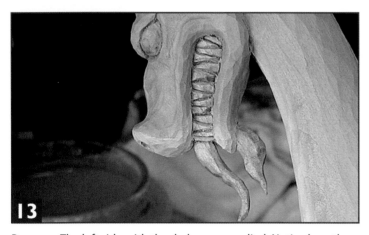

13

Progress: The left side with the dark green applied. Notice how the layering effect helps to create depth.

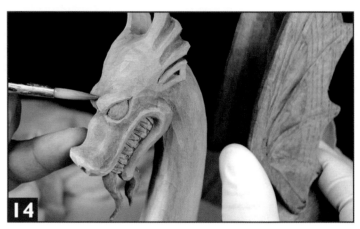

14

Using the ¼" round brush, add the dark green wash to the head area. Rim the lips, deepen the brows, and add tone to the bridge of the snout, as shown.

15

Using the ¾" flat brush, apply a wash coat of olive green to the wings. Paint only the insides and the spines, or top edges of the wings.

16

Using the ¼" flat brush, carefully paint in the "fingers" with olive green.

Using the ¼" flat brush, apply a wash coat of bright yellow to the wings' membranes.

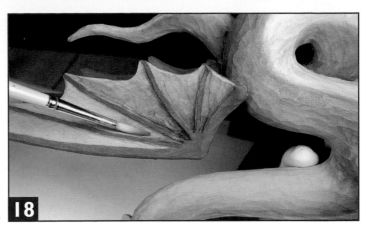

Using the ¼" round brush, layer a small amount of cinnamon over the bright yellow, as shown. Start in the tighter areas of the joints and blend out. Complete both wings.

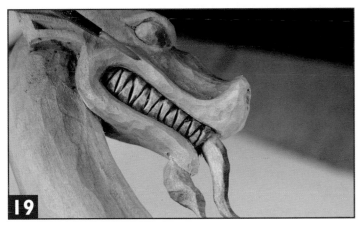

Using a ⅛" round detail brush, rim the teeth with a wash of bright red. This will help to suggest gums.

Using the same brush, paint in the teeth with pure white. Thin the paint just enough to keep it flowing, but not so much that it will bleed into the tiny V-cuts. Paint just the high spots. The low spots will be filled with antique stain, which will make the teeth "pop."

Still using the detail brush, paint the eyeballs with thinned bright yellow.

Apply a small dot of cinnamon to the eyeball to serve as a pupil. Be sure to align each eye—don't make him look cross-eyed!

23

Using the ¼" round brush, apply a wash of mauve to the tongue.

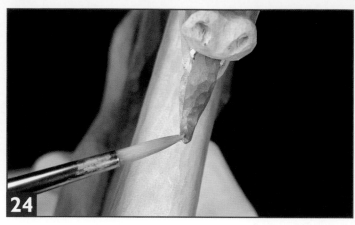

24

Paint the tip of the tongue with a bit of medium purple. Blend it in.

25

With the same brush, paint the Dragon's beard with the olive green.

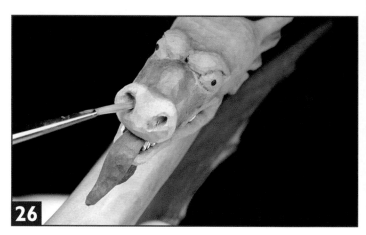

26

Paint in the nostril holes with a bit of mauve on the ⅛" round detail brush.

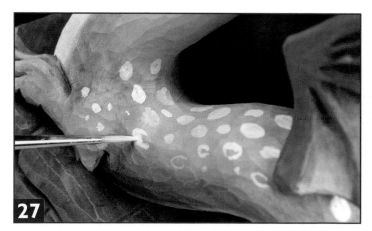

27

Using the detail brush, randomly apply small ovals of thinned mint green along the back of the Dragon. This will suggest scales or markings. Paint them varying sizes; paint some solid, but leave others as outlines.

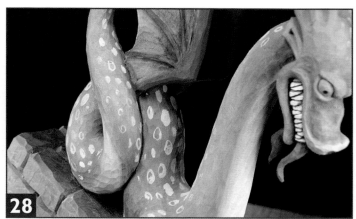

28

Progress: Notice the placement of the applied scales into the twist and on the tail.

29

Apply more scales up the neck and on the forehead.

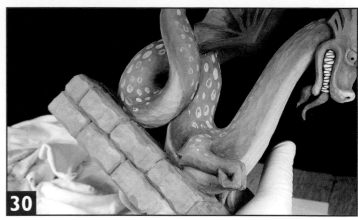

30

Using the ¾" flat brush, apply a wash coat of light gray to the stone wall base. Don't forget the top. Use smaller brushes, such as the ¼" and ⅛" round brushes, to get in around the feet and other tight areas.

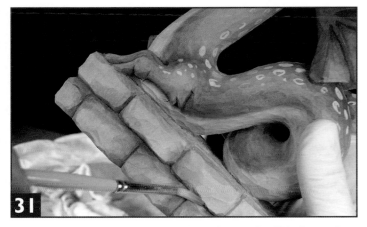

31

Using the ¼" round brush, sparingly apply a wash of black into the seams and cracks of the stone wall, as shown. Painting is complete. Let the carving dry for at least an hour.

32

Seal the carving prior to antiquing. Here I am spraying on a few light coats of fast-drying, clear, matte enamel. It must be matte; the last thing we want is a glossy carving! Let the carving dry overnight.

33

Using a disposable stain brush, apply a brown gel wood stain. Slather it on, working it into the nooks.

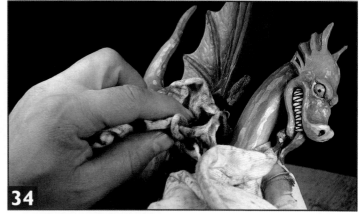

34

Immediately wipe off the excess with a clean cotton rag. Let the carving dry overnight before handling. Your Dragon is complete!

The Unicorn

The unicorn, a symbol of nobility, purity, and innocence, will always be one of the most beautiful creatures ever conceived by the mind of men. "Actual" recorded sightings date back as far as the fourth century, but it wasn't until European Medieval times that belief in unicorns reached its highest peak. It was believed that the horn of the unicorn had magical healing properties and, as a result, was in great demand. So great was the unicorn's skill that hunters could not capture him in chase. Only a pure maiden had the power to ensnare this daring creature; he was drawn to her innocence and would kneel before her and place his head in her lap.

Although the unicorn's origins had him looking like a delicate, goat-like creature, he has transformed into a magnificent equine beauty over the years. My design is more like a horse, with a few differences: a lion's tail, a beard under the chin, and, most obviously, a long spiral horn emerging from his forehead. Also, the sitting position is rather "unhorse-like"; this is uniquely a unicorn's pose.

The provided front and back view patterns are for reference only; you will be cutting the blank from the side view only. The block before sawing will need to measure 7½" x 6" x 2½", and the grain runs vertically. I have mounted the finished carving onto a pre-carved base for stability because the unicorn's delicate features may break if toppled. I chose to keep the base separate; it would be much more difficult to carve between the hind legs if it were kept whole. You may create any type of base you like; I kept mine simple.

Roughing out the carving will require the vise; finer details can be done with the carving in hand, but mind the delicate areas such as the tail and the horn.

The horn is carved separately and glued into a predrilled hole. I carved this horn out of mahogany for added strength.

RIGHT SIDE

GRAIN

© Shawn Cipa

LEFT
SIDE

DRILL
3/16" HOLE

GRAIN

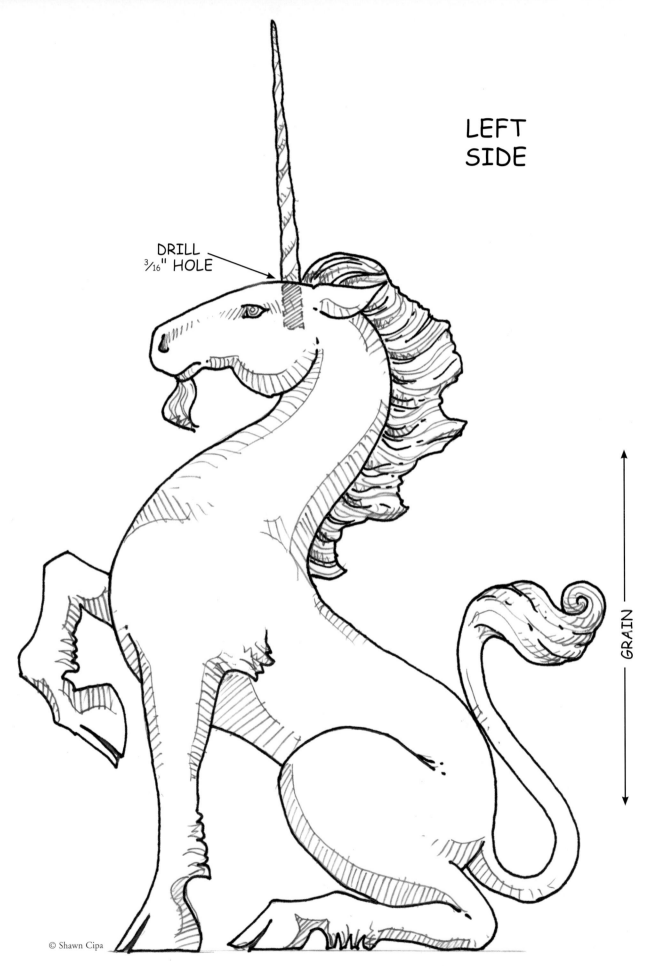

© Shawn Cipa

FRONT

BACK

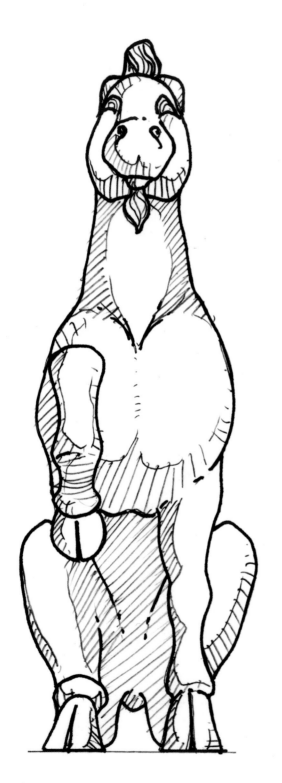

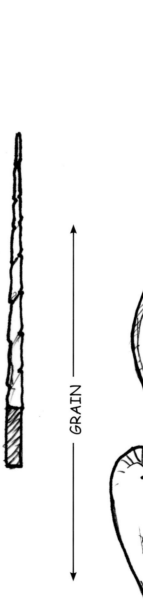

GRAIN

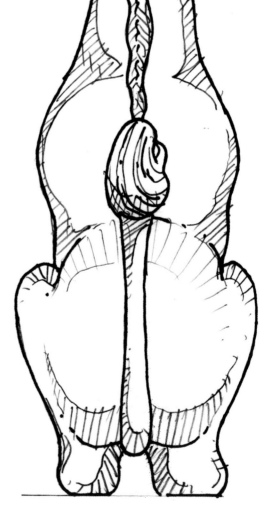

© Shawn Cipa

The Mermaid

In ancient times, mermaids and mermen were considered deities among certain cultures, such as in Greek and Roman mythologies. Many centuries later, they were thought of as elusive but very real creatures. During the early Middle Ages, mermaids were believed to exist, even by the most educated men, and were recorded zoologically. Mermaids were thought to be treacherous to the sailors that spent months at sea; they would lure the sailors to drown by playing music and flaunting their beauty. There have been many recorded sightings of mermaids, as recent as the nineteenth century.

This design is fairly straightforward and compact, with our Mermaid caught in a moment of quiet repose. She is perched upon a rock awaiting an unwary seagoing traveler. The left and right side patterns are for reference only. You will be sawing the blank from the front view only.

The block before sawing measures 8" x 6" x 2½", and the grain runs vertically.

FRONT

GRAIN

© Shawn Cipa

BACK

GRAIN

© Shawn Cipa

RIGHT

LEFT

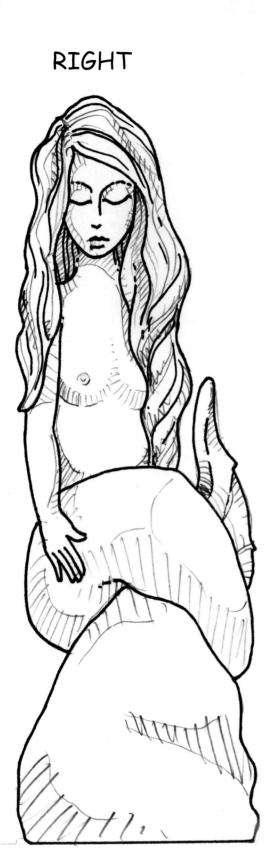

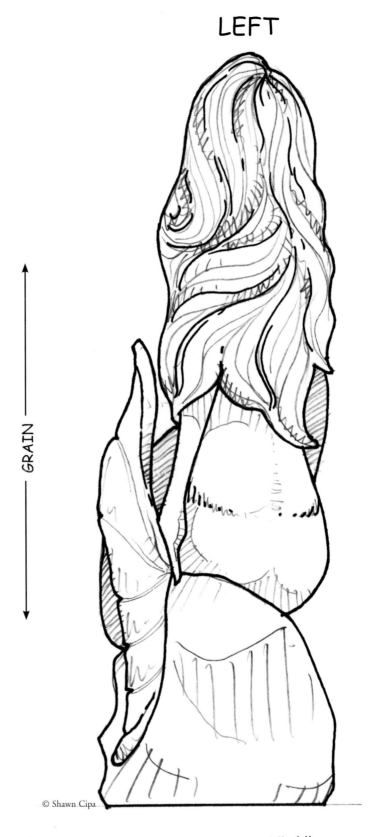

GRAIN

© Shawn Cipa

The Phoenix

The phoenix myth is common legend among many ancient civilizations, but the origin is attributed to the Egyptians and was made more popular by ancient Greece. The phoenix was said to possess a splendid golden-red plumage that made it appear to be wrapped in flames. According to legends, only one phoenix lived at a time and lived for 500 years. At the end of its life cycle, the phoenix built a nest as it was dying and set the nest on fire, being consumed by the flames. After its death, a new phoenix would then arise from the ashes. This cycle would continue over and over. The phoenix was the symbolic representation of death and rebirth or of the setting and rising of the sun.

This design is fairly easy to accomplish. I have shown the bird rising from (or being consumed by) a burst of flame. Again, the carving should be roughed out using a vise and then may be handheld for refinement of its features.

The block before sawing needs to measure 10" x 6" x 2½". The grain runs vertically.

FRONT

GRAIN

© Shawn Cipa

BACK

GRAIN

© Shawn Cipa

The Sorcerer

Like the Wizard, the Sorcerer also is a magician and a wielder of power. However, he is more dark and brooding, with his own ideas at hand. Perhaps he is divining the future with his crystal ball…

The Sorcerer is one of the easier projects in this book. My stylized design depicts an elongated body, with hands only appearing from the robe. The hand holding the crystal ball is part of the whole piece, while the left hand is carved separately. Drill a ¼"-diameter hole for the left hand, as shown in the pattern. When carving the hand, carve a "dowel" opposite of the open palm. Carve it to fit snugly into the ¼" hole. Glue it into place with yellow wood glue.

The pattern needs to be photocopied at 125% to be the size of the project I carved here. It would be even better larger than that, if you would like to experiment. The block before sawing measures 12½" x 4" x 3", and the grain is vertical. The block for the left hand measures 1½" x 1½" x 1". For strength, the grain should run along the length of the fingers.

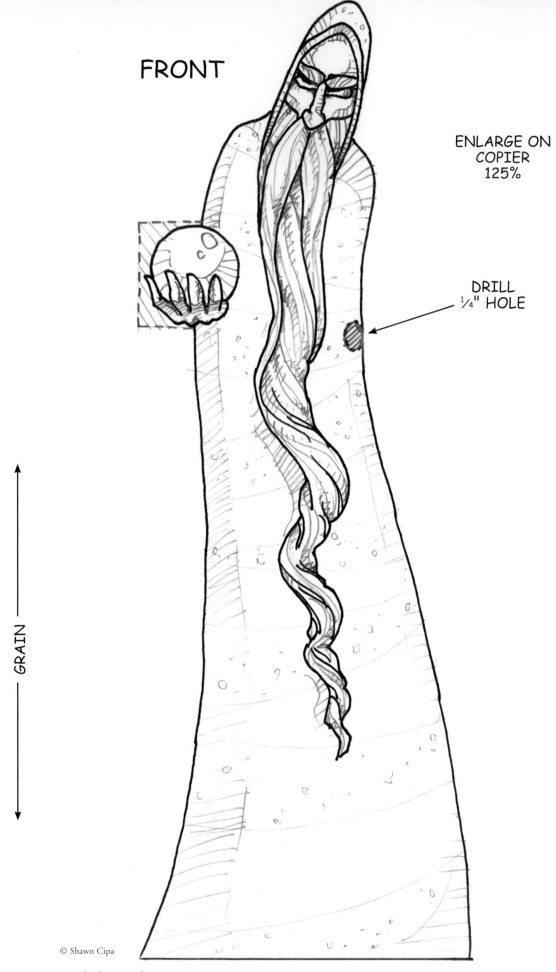

FRONT

ENLARGE ON
COPIER
125%

DRILL
¼" HOLE

GRAIN

© Shawn Cipa

SIDE

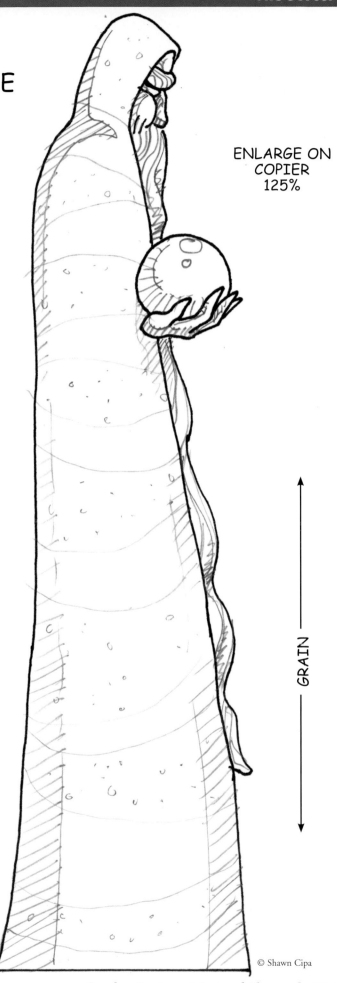

ENLARGE ON
COPIER
125%

GRAIN

LEFT HAND

BOTTOM VIEW OF
RIGHT HAND

© Shawn Cipa

The Sorceress

The Sorceress, the Snow Queen, the White Witch—call her what you will, but beware! She will cast a spell upon you with terrible swiftness. This carving has been inspired by the literary character, the White Witch, from C.S. Lewis's Chronicles of Narnia. She declares herself the Queen of Narnia and has laid all the lands in the midst of an unending winter. Her beauty is surpassed only by her cruelty. Her heart is icy cold.

This carving design is similar to the stylized Sorcerer, with the elongated body and attached hands. Once the body is carved, drill ¼"-diameter holes for the hands, as the pattern shows. The hands are carved separately (mind the grain direction) and glued into place. The right hand will need to have a small ⅛" hole drilled through to accommodate the scepter, or magic wand. The wand is then glued into the hole, as well as to the fingertips of the left hand. This pattern must be photocopied at 125% to be the size of the project I carved here. This carving would also be nice on a much larger scale.

The block before sawing will need to measure 12½"x 4" x 3", with the grain running vertically. The block for the left hand will measure 1¼" x ¾" x 1", while the block for the right hand will measure ¾" x ½" x 1". The scepter should be carved of a harder wood, such as black walnut, in order to give it strength. The blank will measure 4¾" long and ¼" wide.

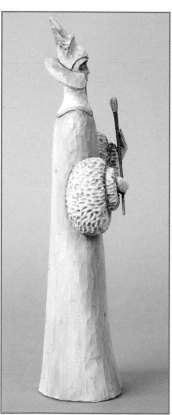

FRONT

ENLARGE ON
COPIER
125%

DRILL
³⁄₈" HOLES
FOR HANDS

GRAIN

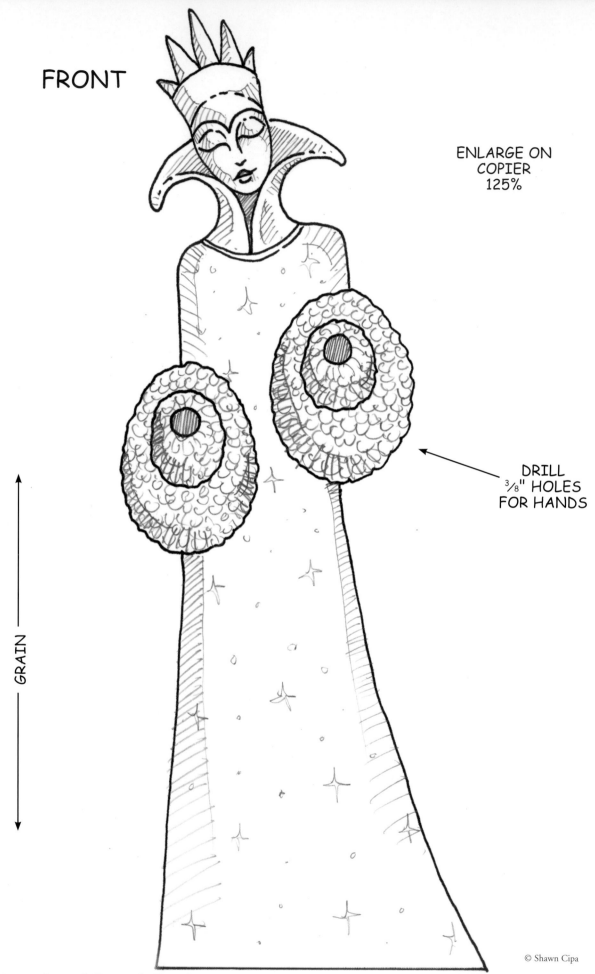

© Shawn Cipa

BACK

ENLARGE ON
COPIER
125%

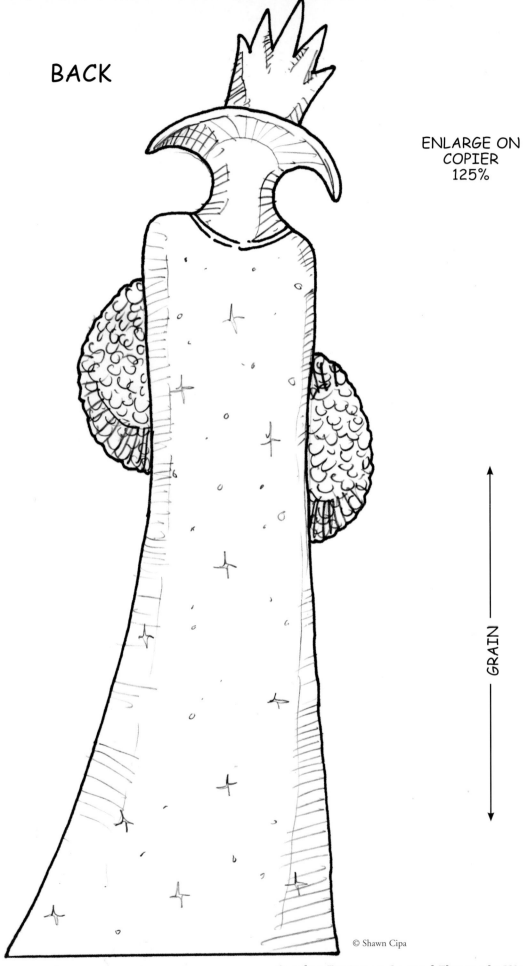

GRAIN

© Shawn Cipa

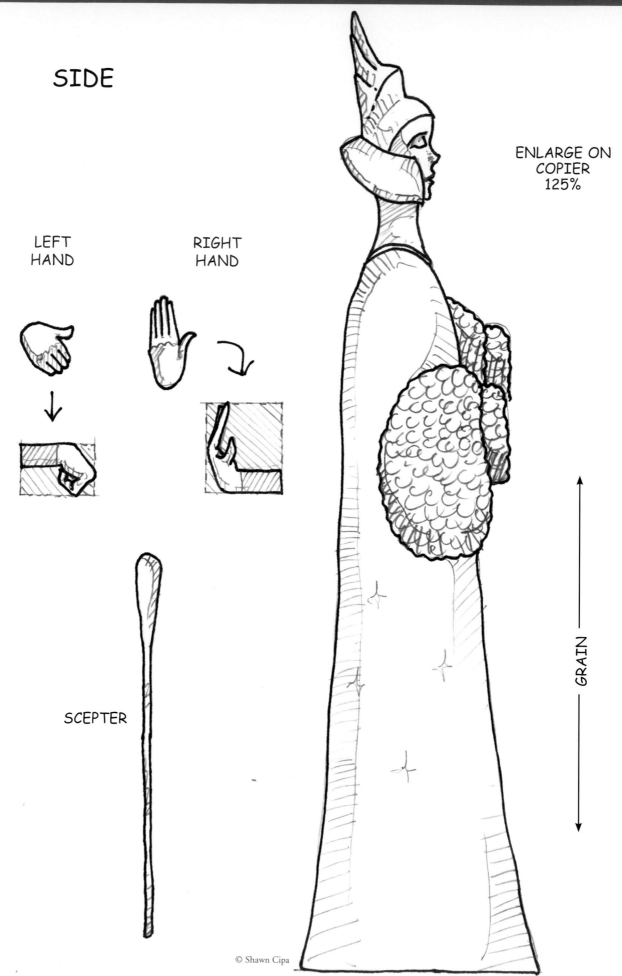

SIDE

LEFT
HAND

RIGHT
HAND

SCEPTER

ENLARGE ON
COPIER
125%

GRAIN

© Shawn Cipa

The Red Dragon

This design is simply an alternative to the prior version of the Dragon. There are similar features, but this guy has powerful back legs, a barbed tail, horns, and wings that are more like a bird's. This is a prime example of how "anything goes," really. You are limited only by your own imagination.

This piece is also an excellent study of form and is great practice in carving around changing grain directions. The rear legs are against each other for strength and simplicity of design. Notice that I have provided a profile of the bottom of the feet, with the toes splayed outward. This provides stability and should not require a base. You could, of course, include a base if you wish.

The block before sawing will need to be 10" x 6" x 2½". The grain runs horizontally, not vertically.

FRONT

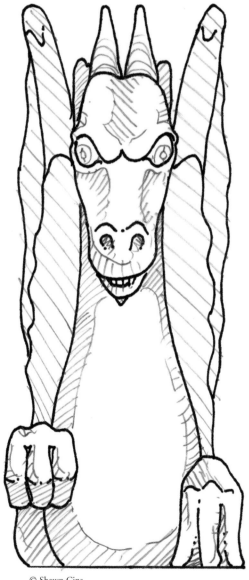

© Shawn Cipa

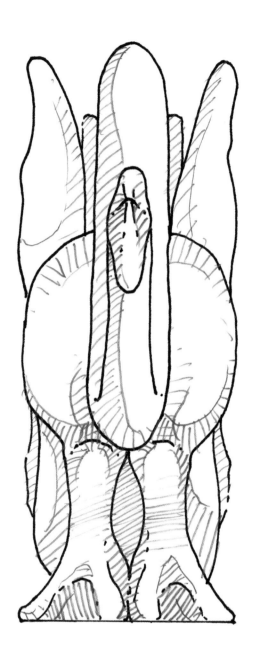

BACK

SIDE

GRAIN

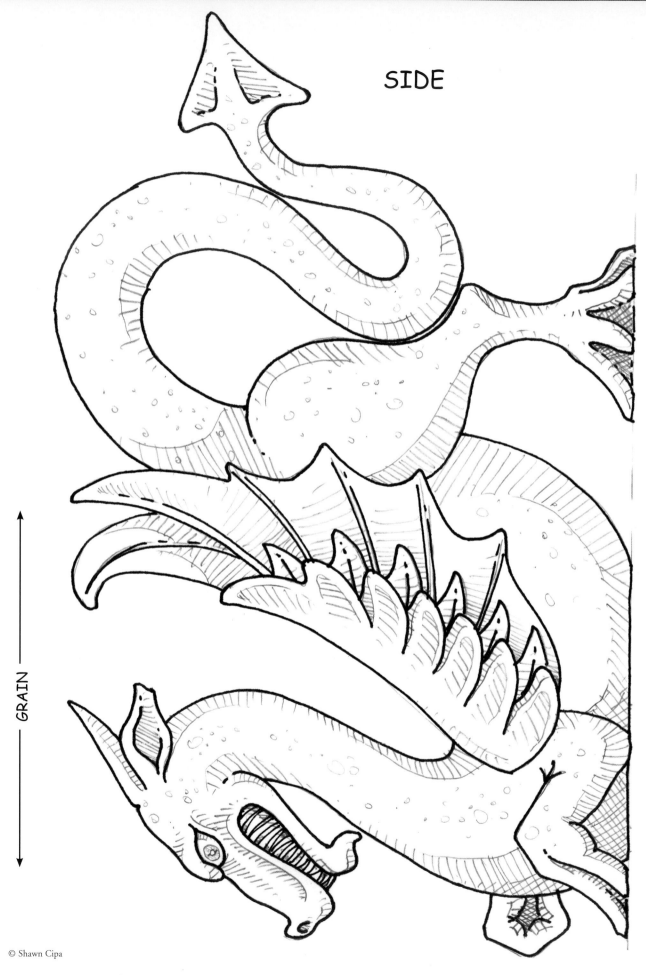

BOTTOM PROFILE
FOR BACK FEET

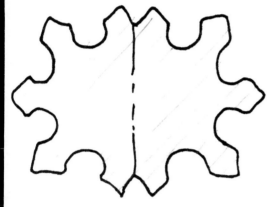

TOP PROFILE
OF HEAD

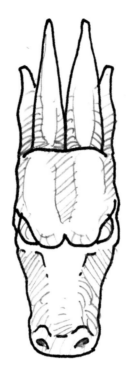

DETAIL OF
RIGHT FOOT

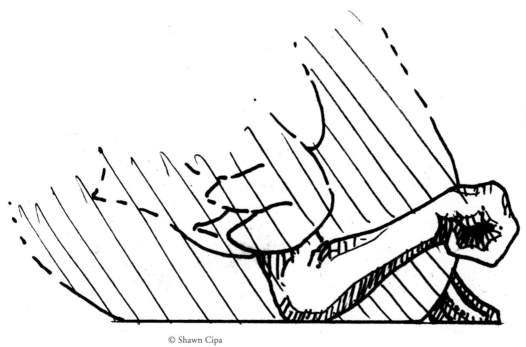

© Shawn Cipa

The Gryphon

The mighty gryphon is actually a composite of two animals. The front is of an eagle's head, talons, and wings, whereas the rear is that of a lion's. Gryphons have long been a symbol of combined strength and intelligence and have adorned many a family crest. An individual gryphon was said to be quite large and could carry a horse and rider off in its talons. Marco Polo claimed to have spotted these fierce beasts during his travels and stated that they were from the mountains of Madagascar, where they hoarded and savagely protected the gold that was mined from the earth there. In reality, he may have actually seen a condor or the extinct elephant bird of Madagascar.

I designed this fellow to stand at attention, with his chest puffed out in pride. Pay special attention to the talons; I have provided a bird's-eye view illustration of his front feet. The area between the front and rear legs is a little difficult to hollow out. Use a drill first to remove the bulk, and then take your time and carve out small bites until the job is complete. The space between the wings can be taken out with a pull saw.

The block before sawing measures 10" x 6" x 2½", and the grain runs vertically.

SIDE

GRAIN

© Shawn Cipa

FRONT

PROFILE FOR
TOP OF HEAD

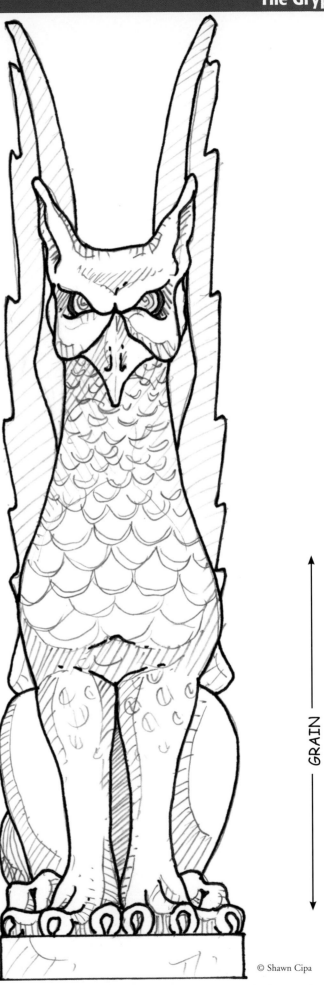

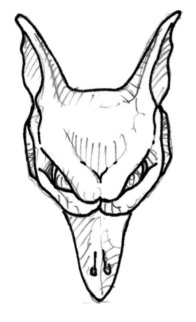

GRAIN

© Shawn Cipa

BACK

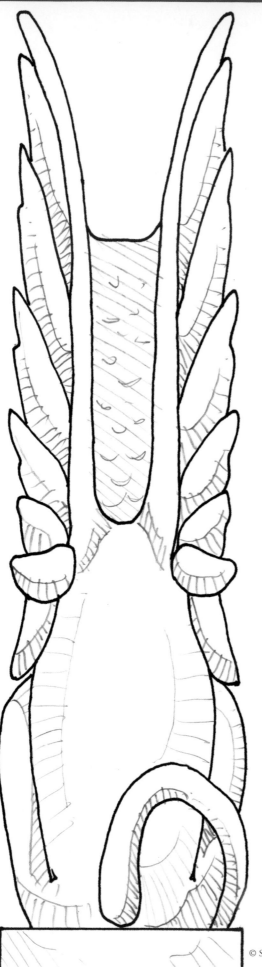

BIRD'S-EYE VIEW
FOR PLACEMENT
OF FEET

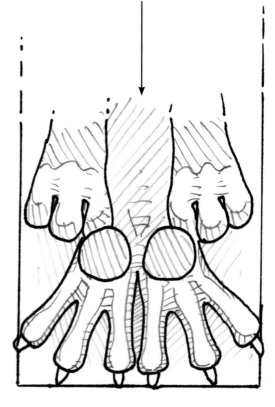

© Shawn Cipa

The Winged Lion

The winged lion has emerged from many a folklore tale, from Mesopotamia (Iraq) to Bali. This majestic beast is also a symbol for Saint Mark in the Roman Catholic Church. It has been included in many modern fantasy stories and is a striking symbol of strength and benevolence.

I have designed the classic statuesque pose: at rest, but alert. The base is part of the carving, as opposed to being a separate piece. A pull saw is very helpful in removing the space between the wings.

The block before sawing measures 8" x 6" x 3", and the grain will run horizontally, as opposed to the more typical vertical situation. This is because it is harder to find basswood stock wider than six inches. You may, of course, laminate two pieces together to get the size you want.

BACK

FRONT

© Shawn Cipa

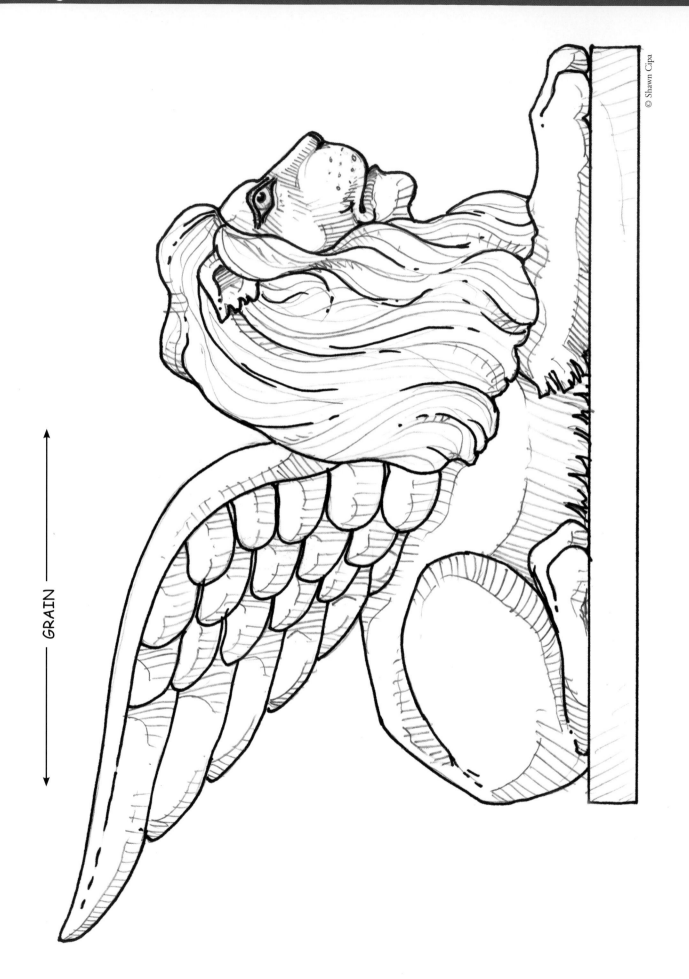

GRAIN

© Shawn Cipa

BIRD'S-EYE VIEW
OF FRONT FEET
PLACEMENT

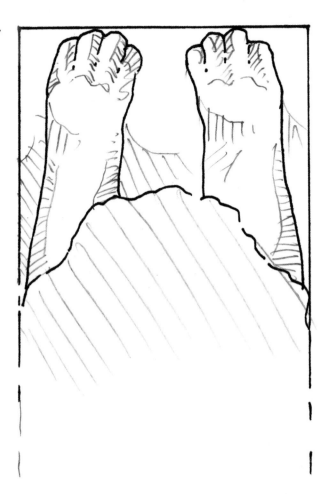

TAIL

© Shawn Cipa

The Seahorse

The sea horse, also called the Hippocamp or Hippocampus in ancient Greece, was the immortal steed that pulled Neptune's chariot through the oceans. The Hippocamp was half horse, half fish. Often used in heraldry and family crests, the Hippocamp is quite the image of nobility.

This design is one of my favorites. It is fairly easy to carve, especially after getting practice from some of the other projects in this book. It requires a base, as shown. I have provided a pattern for the base. Notice how the positioning of the sea horse on the different sized waves tilts his body upward. This makes all the difference in his stance. When attaching the carving to the base, use small nails or pieces of wire as support while gluing.

The block before sawing measures 9½" x 6" x 2", and the grain runs horizontally. The block for the base is 9½" x 4" x 2¼" , and the grain also runs horizontally.

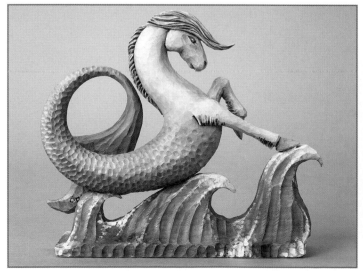

RIGHT
SIDE

GRAIN

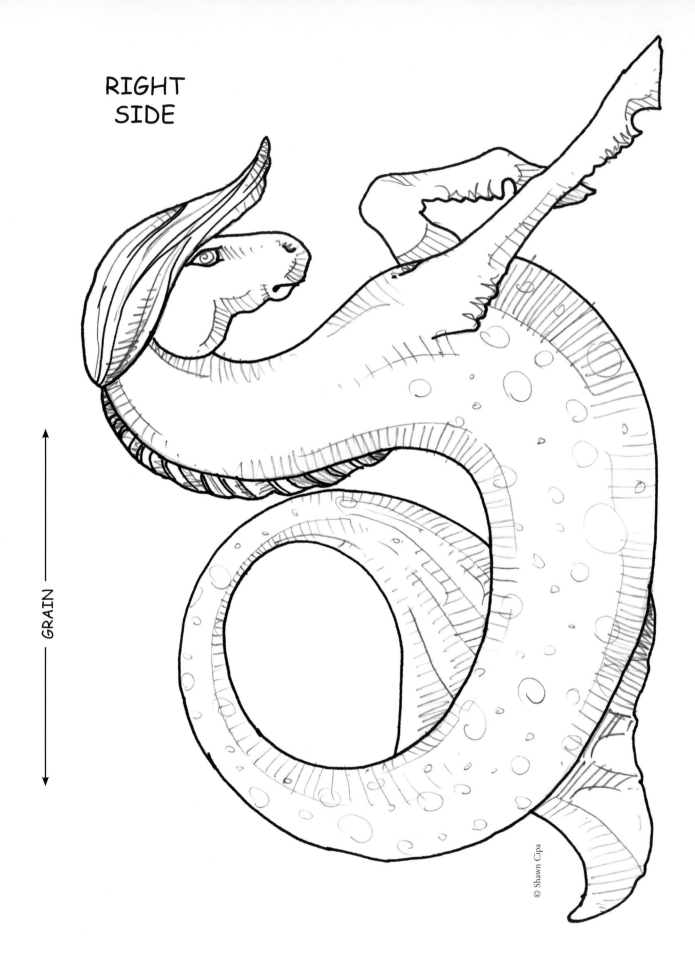

© Shawn Cipa

LEFT
SIDE

© Shawn Cipa

GRAIN

FRONT

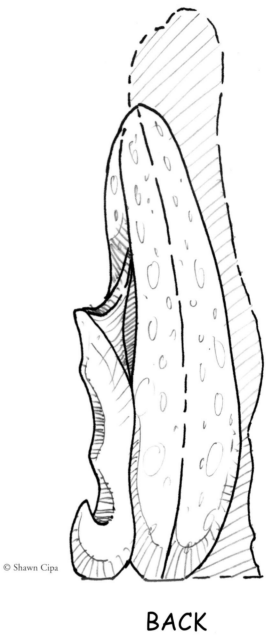

© Shawn Cipa

BACK

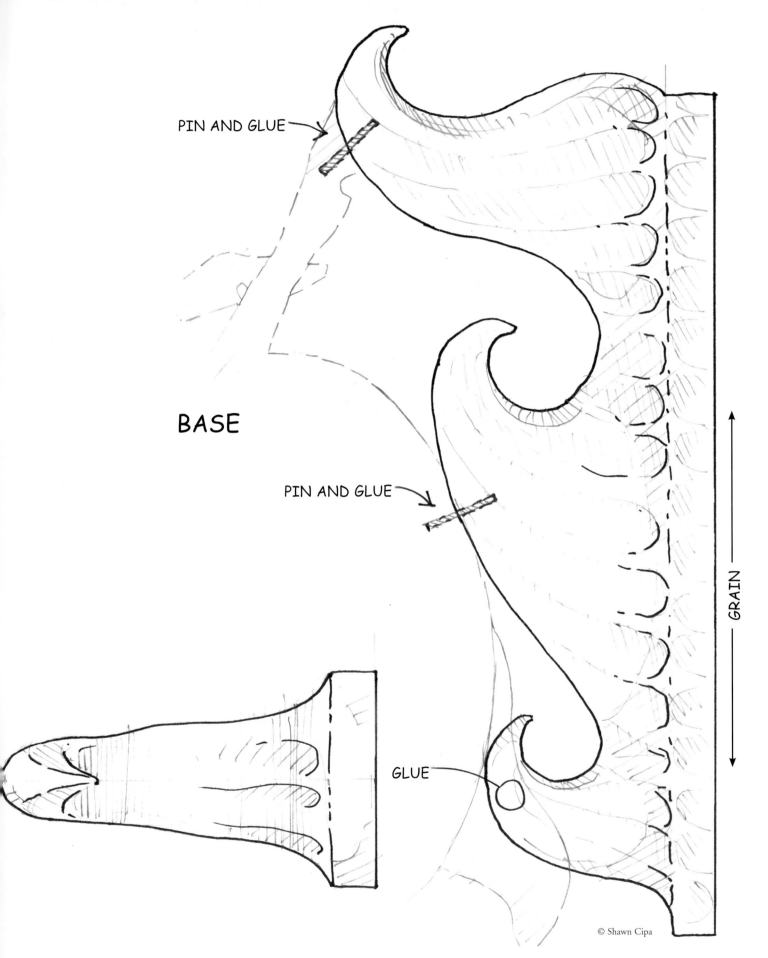

PIN AND GLUE

BASE

PIN AND GLUE

GRAIN

GLUE

© Shawn Cipa

A Little
Green Faerie

Faeries are the denizens of the land of Faerie, an unseen but often felt region that lies "in between" the conscious and the subconscious, the light and the dark, the living and the dead. Faerie lore dates back several millennia and has roots in almost every ancient culture. There are uncountable types and variations of these little folk, so it is impossible to categorize them. They can be helpful, mischievous, benevolent, mean, beautiful, and ugly. Have you ever been suddenly inspired (or repulsed) without quite knowing how or why? It was probably the influence of a faerie.

Our little fellow is your ordinary, garden-variety green faerie; he can be found helping your garden to grow or torturing the family cat. This design was fun to create, and a bit difficult to accomplish. Study the relationship between the front, back, and side patterns carefully before beginning. Take your time and work it out. If things start to go a little differently than the pattern, that's okay—faeries are well known for shape shifting. However your faerie turns out, it will be an original.

The block will have to measure 10" x 6" x 5", and the grain runs vertically.

FRONT

GRAIN

© Shawn Cipa

BACK

GRAIN

© Shawn Cipa

SIDE

GRAIN

© Shawn Cipa